Power and Par........

INTRAC NGO Management and Policy Series

Power and Partnership?

Experiences of NGO Capacity-Building

Edited by

Rick James

INTRAC NGO Management and Policy Series No. 12

An INTRAC Publication

INTRAC:

A Summary Description

INTRAC, the International NGO Training and Research Centre, was set up in 1991 to provide specially designed training, consultancy and research services to organisations involved in international development and relief. Our goal is to improve NGO performance by exploring policy issues and by strengthening management and organisational effectiveness.

First published in 2001 in the UK by
INTRAC
PO Box 563
Oxford
OX2 6RZ
United Kingdom

Tel: +44 (0)1865 201851
Fax: +44 (0)1865 201852
e-mail: intrac@gn.apc.org

ISBN 1-897748-59-0

Designed and produced by
Jerry Burman Associates
Tel: 01803 409754

Printed in Great Britain by
Antony Rowe Ltd., Chippenham, Wiltshire

Foreword

This book is based on the proceedings of the NGO Capacity-Building panel of the 'NGOs in a Global Future Conference' which took place in January 1999 in Birmingham, UK. This was the third international NGO conference since 1992 organised by Mike Edwards and David Hulme, this time with the support of Tina Wallace from the School of Public Policy, Birmingham University. The purpose of this conference was to explore the opportunities for civic action that global trends are creating for NGOs. The conference was organised into thirteen parallel panels which included themes such as: NGOs in a Future without Aid; Role of NGOs in Complex Political Emergencies; Community Economic Development; Building Social Capital; Engendering Organisations; Can Corporations be Civil?; New Directions in Global Advocacy. INTRAC was asked to facilitate the panel on NGO Capacity-Building.

The papers presented in this publication are the majority of those presented at the conference. The IFCB (International Forum on Capacity-Building) hosted one of the sessions, and the synthesis report of their comprehensive capacity-building survey is included in this publication, although it was not directly presented during the workshop. Two of the papers presented in the panel are not included, either because of copy-write or because they were presented as work-in-progress. They were both, however, valuable think-pieces which contributed to the conclusions of this book. Rick James of INTRAC has lightly edited the cases presented and written an introduction and conclusion. The conclusion highlights the key findings from the papers and discusses the resulting implications for international NGOs developing a strategy towards capacity-building.

Acknowledgements

INTRAC would like to thank the conference organisers, Mike Edwards, David Hulme and Tina Wallace for inviting INTRAC to host the capacity-building panel as well as encourage publication of the findings. The conference itself was sponsored by DFID; SIDA; and the Swiss Agency for Development and Cooperation. Support to individual participants was received from Charity Projects and the British Council. The time for writing up this publication was generously sponsored by the 'proactive' group of INTRAC international NGO supporters.

INTRAC would particularly like to thank the presenters at the panel Margaret Mwaura of CORAT Kenya; Rachel Roland of CDS, UK; Rasha Omar of CRDT, Egypt; Raj Patel of Opportunity International in India; Roy Trivedy of SCF in Mozambique; John Hailey from Oxford Brookes University, UK; Gavin Andersson from Development Resource Centre in South Africa; and Anne Garbutt from INTRAC presenting about Central Asia. We are grateful to them for writing up their presentations as case studies. We would also like to thank Rajesh Tandon of PRIA and David Brown of IDR for allowing publication of the excellent IFCB Report. Joyce Mataya from Malawi deserves special mention for her Lomadef case study in the chapter on organisation development.

Other individuals have contributed in terms of reading and commenting on drafts: Brian Pratt, Liz Goold, Alan Fowler, John Hailey, Vicky Brehm, Max Lawson and Cathy have all provided useful guidance and input. Thank you too to Carolyn Blaxall for coordinating the actual publication and Marie G Diaz for copy-editing.

To Dad and Mum – for all you have taught me about 'capacity-building' which empowers.

Contents

Abbreviations

AD	Allied Dunbar
AD/ZFS	Allied Dunbar/Zurich Financial Services
CDRA	Community Development Resource Association
CDS	Centre for Development Services
CORAT	Christian Organisations Research Advisory Trust
CRDT	Centre for Rural Development and Training
DFID	Department for International Development
EASUN	East Africa Support for NGOs
GAD	Gender and Development
HRD	Human Resource Development
IDR	Institute for Development Research
IFCB	International Forum on Capacity-Building
INGO	International NGO
NEF	New Economics Foundation
NGO	Non-Government Organisation
NGOSO	NGO Support Organisation
NNGO	Northern NGO
OD	Organisation Development
ODC	OD Consultancy
OI	Opportunity International
PRA	Participative Rural Appraisal
PRIA	Society for Participative Research in Asia
SCF	Save the Children Fund
SNGO	Southern and Eastern NGO
TOT	Training of Trainers
WID	Women in Development

Introduction

What is Capacity-Building?

The term 'capacity-building' has become almost synonymous with 'development' in many aid circles. The World Bank, bilateral and multilateral donors, international NGOs (INGOs) and some local NGOs are prioritising capacity-building. A recent survey of Northern NGOs revealed that an overwhelming majority, over 91%, claimed to be involved in capacity-building[1]. It is therefore critical to analyse carefully the practice of capacity-building to ensure that we learn from others' experience and avoid the danger that the term capacity-building becomes merely a cosmetic and meaningless addition to all proposals and policies. Capacity-building is a conscious approach to change which, if taken seriously, has very radical and far-reaching implications not only for skills and behaviours, but also power dynamics within and between organisations.

This book seeks to contribute to our understanding of capacity-building by analysing a number of specific capacity-building interventions, drawing out the issues and insights from practice. It also highlights the consequent implications, particularly for Northern NGOs involved in developing strategies for capacity-building. It is aimed at all development professionals engaged in capacity-building, but has particular relevance to Northern NGOs, Southern NGOs and capacity-building providers.

It has emerged out of the 1999 NGO Conference, 'NGOs in a Global Future' in Birmingham, UK. Within this conference a panel was set up to focus on NGO capacity-building. Individuals were invited to present papers describing their actual experiences of NGO capacity-building, in order to understand better how capacity-building is implemented in practice, what actually happens, what works and why. This publication is a synthesis of some of the papers presented.

[1] R. James, et al., 1998, 'Survey of Northern NGO Approaches to Capacity-Building', IWGCB.

1

STRUCTURE OF PUBLICATION

This book seeks to redress the imbalance in capacity-building literature, by beginning with a Southern articulation of NGO capacity-building issues and priorities. The second part looks at capacity-building at the level of individual people and organisations: a description of leadership development training in churches in Africa is presented by Margaret Mwaura of CORAT, and the common elements and key success factors of an OD intervention are outlined by Rick James (with Joyce Mataya). Part III provides some cases of mutual capacity-building or capacity-building by 'partnership'. Rachel Roland and Rasha Omar describe a capacity-building linkage programme between two institutions (one in the UK and one from Egypt) and Raj Patel outlines the process of 'reverse capacity-building' between Northern and Southern and Eastern institutions. Part IV examines two different interventions which focus on capacity-building at a societal level. Roy Trivedy presents an example of developing a social movement in Mozambique and Anne Garbutt describes a multilevel capacity-building programme in Central Asia. The final part seeks to draw lessons from the cases informing such questions as:

- What capacity-building **needs** are identified by the Southern NGOs themselves?
- What is the impact of the **context** on the capacity-building intervention?
- What actually comprises **capacity-building interventions**?
- What **principles of good practice** for capacity-building interventions emerge?
- What are the links between capacity-building and **programme impact** with beneficiaries?
- How do **power dynamics** affect **partnership** in capacity-building?

The book concludes with implications and pointers for Northern NGOs in **developing capacity-building strategies**.

Before examining the cases presented and drawing lessons, it is important to clarify to some degree the term 'capacity-building'.

WHAT IS CAPACITY-BUILDING?

This most obvious question continues to elude a consensual definition. Capacity-building is certainly difficult to clearly define and is resistant to 'one right answer'. To some degree this lack of clarity is exacerbated by the incentive to use capacity-building to mean whatever one wants it to as it currently carries 'weight' with donors. As a result, capacity-building is becoming such an over-used phrase as to render it almost meaningless.

Two definitions which INTRAC has found useful are as follows:

Capacity-building is an ongoing process of helping people, organisations and societies improve and adapt to changes around them. Performance and improvements are taken in the light of the mission, objectives, context, resources and sustainability.

Organisational capacity-building is a conscious intervention to improve an organisation's effectiveness and sustainability in relation to its mission and context.

The first definition highlights the ongoing nature of capacity-building and the different levels to which it can apply. The second definition focuses on the organisational level and highlights that it is a conscious or explicit (rather than accidental) intervention. As Huse and Cummings state, 'although change is inevitable, change that happens to an organisation can be distinguished from change that is planned by organisational members' [2]. Both definitions recognise that the mission has to be contextualised and that effectiveness is not necessarily sustainable. Neither definition considers whether capacity-building is an 'outside' intervention in an organisation's life or whether capacity can be built internally. While most capacity-building interventions do tend to be external, it is important to realise that this is not exclusively the case as organisations are also able to build their capacity from within to some degree.

INTRAC has also found two basic frameworks that are useful in understanding the concept of capacity-building, accepting that while 'all models are wrong, some are useful'.

LEVELS OF CAPACITY-BUILDING

Capacity-building can occur at different levels and it is important to clearly define which is meant to avoid confusion (there are a number of different ways of applying this model and it is common to add communities and community groups).

The cases presented in this publication illustrate a number of these different levels. For development agencies it becomes a strategic choice to make – at which level(s) are we trying to concentrate our efforts to build capacity. By

[2] E. Huse and T. Cummings, 1985, *Organization Development and Change.*

drawing the levels as concentric circles but only with dotted lines, the interrelationship between them is clearly visible. There is no one right answer about which level to concentrate on – they are all important in their different ways and a change in one has an impact up or down the levels.

Another model which has proved useful to some for understanding the different dimensions of capacity-building is the **INTRAC Clover Leaf Model**.

In this simple model NGOs are viewed as an interlocking combination of three main areas: their programmes; their internal organisation and their external linkages - all within a certain context. In this model the internal divisions between the three main elements have been withdrawn to emphasise the extent of the overlap and interrelationship between them.

In the past capacity-building has largely concentrated on the programme circle. Developmental problems were seen as primarily technical and most capacity-building needs were defined as an absence of technical training in the NGO's programme staff. The link between capacity-building and programme output was very clear and close.

More recently there has been a recognition of the limitations of this programme-focused approach. Despite the technical training, NGO performance has continued to be disappointing. Many NGO projects fail to deliver, not

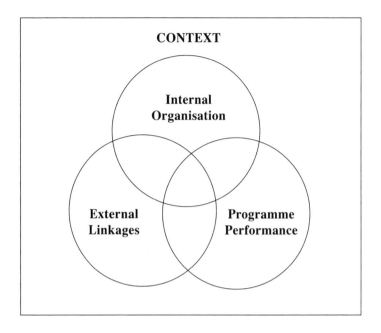

because of poorly conceived technical projects, but because there was not the necessary leadership or staffing to make things happen. This has led to a shift in focus to organisational factors needing 'capacity-building' with an emphasis on internal issues such as NGO leadership, culture, strategy, systems, structures and resources.

Most recently the influence of external relations on the impact of NGOs' work has been increasingly seen. NGOs are recognising that in isolation they cannot bring development and that they are merely one actor amongst a wide array of different stakeholders. If NGOs are to be effective in fostering development, they need to relate well to other actors. They may need to: influence national or local government decisions; gain from the experience of other organisations and avoid reinventing the wheel; and co-operate systematically with other institutions if their own objectives are to be met.

Similarly too with the 'contextual' box. Rather than merely framing this model, the context is increasing seen as a critical and pervasive factor in determining capacity-building needs and appropriate interventions. To a large extent, it has been changes in the context that have created the need for capacity-building. It is obvious that the success of many capacity-building interventions is highly dependent on the context.

When discussing 'what is capacity-building' it is essential to realise that capacity exists independent of any external capacity-building effort. Many capacity-building programmes in the past have failed by concentrating merely on the capacity problems which exist rather than looking for the potential and building on the existing capacity. This point is reflected in the ongoing debate about the appropriateness of the term capacity-building as 'building' tends to imply starting something from scratch. Alternative terms such as capacity enhancement; capacity growth; capacity strengthening and capacity development have been put forward and are used internally by a variety of agencies. None of these alternatives has managed to dislodge 'capacity-building' from its number one slot and it is still the most widely used description today. While the reasons for finding an alternative are good ones, they may have failed to gain widespread acceptance perhaps simply because they are cumbersome, or because of the subconscious attraction implicit in 'we are building something'. Rather than debate which term is most appropriate it seems sensible to go with the most popular term and spend more time trying to understand what it means.

WHAT IS THE PURPOSE OF CAPACITY-BUILDING?

The purpose of capacity-building can be said to be twofold: first, to address the internal weaknesses that NGOs experience and to build on their strengths; and second, to help them adjust to the rapidly changing external environment. The ultimate reason for doing this is so that programme performance – impact at beneficiary level – can improve.

In developing capacity-building programmes much attention has been given to the first reason with considerable analysis of common NGO problems. The second reason for building capacity has received less attention and merits some consideration here in order to get a global overview before descending into the gritty details of specific capacity-building programmes. According to Alan Fowler, there are major global trends in the aid sector which influence the nature of capacity-building[3] and make it different today. These trends include:

- globalisation which results in accelerating change and opening of new markets over which governments have less and less control;
- the support for the emergence of civil society as a countervailing power to the state
- decentralisation from national to local governments;
- a proliferation of NGOs fed by availability of financial resources from donors and by the retrenchment of staff from the civil service;

[3] A. Fowler, Jan. 2000, presentation at INGO Training programme, Arusha, Tanzania.

- the changing aid agenda – in the past aid used to be given on the basis of political 'spheres of influence'; now aid is given to ensure 'stability' since poverty and exclusion are destabilising factors which add to migration pressures on the North;
- the declining levels of overall aid (a 29% fall in real terms between 1991–1997) while increasing funding for NGOs.

All these trends have very real implications for NGO capacity-building as they may lead to a greater demand for NGO services; a pressure to be involved in more service delivery; the need to be more involved in advocacy; the need to establish more trust through values and integrity; and challenges to the very identity of NGOs. These trends place new capacity-building demands on NGOs and raise the question, what are you building NGO capacity to do?

We now must see how NGO capacity-building programmes are responding in practice.

Part One

Capacity-Building Needs

Voices from the South

Chapter 1

Southern NGO Capacity-Building: Issues and Priorities

International Forum On Capacity-Building of Southern NGOs

A Synthesis of Consultations and Surveys with Southern NGOs, Northern NGOs and Donor Institutions[4]

To date, the capacity-building agenda has been almost exclusively shaped by the North. Northern agencies have been the ones to define the need for NGO capacity-building and also design appropriate solutions to 'other peoples' problems'. Southern NGOs have tended to be largely excluded from the process except as 'passive' recipients of such interventions. The programmes have been driven and owned by Northern agencies and in many cases imposed on Southern agencies as a precondition for funding. And yet it surprises us that the impact of much of NGO capacity-building remains limited!

To address this issue and redress the imbalance, three Southern NGO representatives to the NGO Working Group on the World Bank proposed the creation of an International Working Group on Capacity-Building for Southern NGOs (IWGCB) in late 1996. This would provide a forum for the articulation of Southern perspectives on NGO capacity-building within a wider stakeholder context of multilateral agencies, bilateral development organisations, foundations, and Northern NGOs.

This publication takes the synthesis report of the initiative as its starting point as INTRAC believes it is essential that Southern articulation of Southern NGO capacity-building needs and priorities is a prerequisite for effective impact.

---

[4] Prepared by: Interim Steering Committee. Secretariat: Society for Participatory Research in Asia (PRIA), 42 Tughlakabad Institutional Area, New Delhi 110 062 India
Tel: 698-1908/698 9559 Fax: 9111 698 0183

INTRODUCTION

Over the last decade there has been increasing recognition of the important role for non-governmental development organisations (NGOs) and other agencies of civil society in catalysing and sustaining grass-roots development, particularly in 'Southern' (and Eastern), developing country contexts. The expanding roles of Southern NGOs (SNGOs) have required building their technical, managerial and organisational capacities to carry out complex programmes and to deal effectively with other actors, such as other civil society organisations, governments or businesses.

There is widespread agreement about the importance of capacity-building amongst Northern donor agencies, Northern development NGOs and Southern NGOs themselves. There is less consensus about what capacities are most important or how they can be effectively developed. Southern NGOs see Northern practice as far behind its rhetoric in capacity-building; the services offered often seem tailored to the interests and needs of the Northern provider rather than the Southern recipients. Much capacity-building in the past has been designed to train individuals rather than to foster effective organisations or promote strong civil societies. Too often the design and time perspectives of programmes have not encouraged sustainable local institutions, so benefits have been transitory. In addition, capacity-building services have been offered without prior consultation with recipients, hence services have not been informed by felt needs.

In October, 1996, three Southern NGO representatives to the NGO Working Group on the World Bank proposed the creation of an International Working Group on Capacity-Building for Southern NGOs (IWGCB) that could provide a forum for many different stakeholders – Southern NGOs, multilateral agencies, bilateral development organisations, foundations, Northern NGOs and others – to share perspectives on capacity-building, identify needed programmes and ensure that many voices were heard in developing policies and priorities for future initiatives.

Participants in that initial meeting agreed that there was an important niche to be filled by such an institution. Representatives of the NGO Working Group on the World Bank, the World Bank NGO Division and the USAID Office of Private and Voluntary Co-operation agreed to help organise a meeting of a broader range of stakeholders to explore the idea further and to survey capacity-building donors – foundations, bilateral agencies and multilateral development actors – to develop better understanding of current practices and emerging priorities.

In May 1997 an initial conference of about forty representatives of those stakeholders met at the World Bank in Washington. Participants agreed that the concept had merit in principle. They were particularly concerned that such an institution would enable more attention to Southern voices in decisions about capacity-building priorities and policies. The meeting authorised an Interim Steering Committee to collect and synthesise information about capacity-building priorities from Southern and Northern NGOs to supplement the survey of donors. Those data would provide a basis for discussions of future priorities and policies at an IWGCB Conference in Brussels on 6–8 May, 1998.

The Committee organised a multi-pronged approach designed to provide comparable information while remaining sensitive to varying preferences among stakeholders about data collection and analysis. Teams were organised to collect data from stakeholder groups:

- Southern NGOs in Africa, Asia and Latin America. Separate reports are available from Africa (Eastern and Southern, Horn sub-regions), Asia (South, Southeast sub-regions), and Latin America/Caribbean regions;
- Northern NGOs in North America, Europe and Asia-Pacific;
- foundations, bilateral and multilateral agencies in North America, Europe, and Asia-Pacific.

This synthesis provides brief summaries of the findings from the stakeholder groups. It further compares the priorities and issues that emerged across the stakeholder groups. More detailed analysis of regional concerns is offered in regional and sub-regional reports. This synthesis seeks to identify themes that have significance across many countries and regions.

METHODS FOR JOINT LEARNING

This data collection activity is part of an ongoing learning process that is intended more to develop dialogue and mutual understanding than to identify definitive answers to the questions posed. The processes of collective reflection, within and between stakeholder groups, are probably more important that any specific results generated. We have tried to organise flexible data collection processes that can be adapted to the preferences and styles of the various stakeholders.

The data collection has been carried out by organisations and networks from the target stakeholder groups at the request of the Interim Steering Committee. African, Asian and Latin American NGO support organisations have organised the data collection and analysis processes for Southern NGOs; a committee of bilateral and multilateral donor representatives worked on the donor analysis and an alliance of Northern NGOs carried out the Northern NGO analysis. The data collection strategies used by different stakeholder groups have included a combination of questionnaires, interviews and group consultations, depending on their assessment of the processes most likely to produce sound information. The data have been analysed by a range of tools as well, from statistical analyses of questionnaire data to qualitative analysis of interview results to collective reflections and consultations with groups of stakeholders.

This inquiry has had some surprising consequences. We had expected that consultations might produce new insights and consensus about issues amongst Southern NGOs. We did not anticipate, however, that these reflections would lead to ongoing discussions among participants. In South Asia, for example, participants in the regional consultation agreed to continue discussions and active initiatives on the issue independent of the IWGCB (now called IFCB). In Latin America, the organising networks agreed to make collective reflections on capacity-building the centre-piece of their annual meetings. The consultation process seems to have catalysed ongoing discussions that are appropriating the issue of capacity-building on behalf of Southern NGOs that have often been relatively passive targets of Northern-dominated programmes.

CAPACITY-BUILDING AND DIFFERENT CONSTITUENCIES

Different regions and constituency groups have often focused on different issues, so full understanding of their discussions requires consulting their separate reports. In addition, the data collection processes vary across regions and sub-regions. What is offered here are short summaries of some issues that emerged in different stakeholder analyses.

Southern NGOs: Perspectives of Capacity-Building Recipients

In most regions the basic process involved sharing an initial list of priorities and concerns, and inviting NGOs in national, sub-regional and regional consultations to amend those lists to reflect their views. The process as initially conceived included three steps:

1. national meetings, often via NGO associations, to develop shared lists of capacity-building priorities and lists of benefits and issues associated with North-South NGO co-operation,
2. regional meetings of representatives to develop region-wide lists and analyses, and
3. regional reports by organisers to summarise critical issues and concerns.

In practice, different regions amended the basic process to reflect their particular concerns and interests.

Asian NGOs

In Asia separate data collection and analysis processes were carried out in South Asia and in Southeast Asia. The South Asian region followed the model as outlined above. The sub-regional meeting followed national meetings of NGO communities in Bangladesh, Nepal, Pakistan, Sri Lanka and India (several meetings). The subregional report provided data from country as well as subregional analyses. More than 250 NGOs participated in this series of discussions. The Southeast Asian region used a two-day regional consultation that developed its own issues and frameworks. Seventeen NGOs from five countries – Cambodia, Indonesia, Philippines, Thailand, Vietnam – participated in this consultation.

The South Asia consultations described their deliberations in the 'Politics of Capacity-Building'. This report considers the meaning of capacity-building, the importance of a broad, Southern-based analysis informing its delivery, priorities for capacity-building, the processes by which it is carried out, the role of North-South collaboration, follow-up commitments by participating NGOs and recommendations for the IFCB. Several issues raised by the South Asian subregion may have resonance in other regions as well. For example, the South Asian consultation argued that capacity-building must develop capacity for critical reflection, learning, documentation and dissemination, and that it must be a continuous learning process that enhances accomplishment of the goals and strategies of the organisations and individuals involved. The South Asian NGOs also articulated several additions to the initial list of priorities, including knowledge of environmental, human rights and diversity issues, skills for conflict management, developing entrepreneurs, building communication skills, building peoples' organisations and increasing control over productive resources. South Asian NGOs became committed to continuing reflection and dialogue about capacity-building in the course of these discussions.

The Southeast Asia consultation brought together representatives from diverse NGOs, ranging from grass-roots organisations to advocacy organisations to civil society foundations. They spent their first day on the issue of capacity-building, and concluded that capacity-building needs varied considerably depending on the targets (e.g. individual, organisations) and the capacities in questions (e.g. empowering communities, working with governments). Participants in the consultation emphasised the importance of tailoring the capacity-building activities to civil society and grass-roots needs. They also emphasised the differences in needs of countries at different stages of the evolution of civil society: some countries with well developed civil society organisations were concerned with advocacy and work with governments; others with less experienced NGO communities were wary of government contacts. On the second day of the consultation, NGO participants focused on the actors, goals, values and processes of capacity-building co-operation, especially across sectoral (government, business) and national (North-South, South-South) boundaries. Themes in these discussions included the importance of more South-South co-operation, the growing importance of information technology, the effects of globalisation and the need for intersectoral work by NGOs.

African NGOs
In Africa data collection and analysis activities were undertaken with Southern NGOs in two sub-regions, the Horn of Africa and Eastern and Southern Africa. Similar activities were also planned for West African NGOs, but were not completed in time for this report. In the Horn of Africa, regional priorities were identified on the basis of input from SNGOs in both national and regional consultations. Eventually 21 NGOs from five countries – Eritrea, Ethiopia, Djibouti, Somalia, and Sudan – contributed to the discussions. In Southern and Eastern Africa, input from 48 NGOs in six countries – Botswana, Kenya, Malawi, Tanzania, Uganda and Zambia – has been used to create a preliminary regional report. The report is based on responses to a questionnaire survey and consultations in Kenya, Tanzania and Uganda.

The participants in the Horn of Africa consultations identified major concerns with financial resources, especially the lack of core funding on which NGOs could base their own development. NGOs in the sub-region felt severely constrained by their lack of resources; their dependence on governments and international NGOs for resources was experienced as a threat to their independence and a constraint on their ability to develop their own programmes. They also reported high priority needs for capacity-building to enhance planning and strategic management, programme design and implementation, staff development and other basic organisational capacities. SNGOs from the Horn thought the issues of North-South partnership were fundamental to capacity-building, since most capacity-building programmes are carried out by Northern NGO intermediaries. Southern NGOs valued the mutual learning and increasing programme and organisational capacity possible from such co-operation, but they were acutely aware of their problems of organisational dependence and the difficulties of establishing mutual trust and respect. Over the last two decades the response to humanitarian emergencies in the Horn has created one of the highest concentrations of Northern NGOs in Africa, and many see Northern capacity-building programmes as driven more by Northern needs than by the needs of local NGOs. Programmes that are sensitive to local needs are viewed as essential to creating genuine partnerships, more effective NGOs and sustainable development in the region.

In the six countries of Eastern and Southern Africa, NGO representatives reported a dramatic convergence of capacity-building priorities. In all six countries, leadership development was rated as one of the top three priorities for the future. Leadership in this context refers both to strengthening the leadership skills of existing leaders and to developing the next generation of NGO leaders. The need was particularly acute for new organisations, and for countries in which few if any relevant leadership programmes are currently available. Strategic planning and management was another area in which NGOs saw great need for capacity-building. Participants in these discussions criticised 'pre-packaged' capacity-building programmes that did not involved recipients in programme design and were not responsive to SNGO concerns or lifecycles. Most of these SNGOs were concerned with relationships to Northern NGOs that provided financial resources, and resource transfer issues shaped and coloured all aspects of the relationship. The issue of establishing mutual trust and respect is seen as very important here as well. The consultations indicated that no single definition of the concept of capacity-building is widely shared. Continuing discussions of capacity-building priorities and strengthening regional agencies to provide locally relevant programmes are both essential for the future.

Latin American NGOs

The process for data collection and analysis in the Latin American and Caribbean region involved initial inputs on future capacity-building priorities from 37 NGOs in eleven countries in three regions. NGOs have participated in providing initial data from four countries (Venezuela, Bolivia, Peru and Colombia) in the Andes sub-region, three countries (El Salvador, Costa Rica and Panama) in the Central America and Caribbean sub-region and four countries (Brazil, Uruguay, Argentina and Chile) in the Southern Cone.

This process identified both needs for capacity-building and resources available to meet those needs in the regions. The most widely emphasised needs included fund-raising, monitoring and evaluation and organisation development and renewal. Participants also emphasised the importance of capacity for inter-sectoral relations with government agencies and with business, and the need for staff development programmes. Many participants were also able to identify national and regional resources to respond to many of these concerns, though others were not aware of those resources. Unlike some of the other regions, there appears to be a wide range of resources available for capacity-building initiatives in Latin America and the Caribbean.

The Latin American regional networks that facilitated the collection and analyses of these data have decided that the regional and national dialogues about capacity-building are very important for the future, and for influencing the course of future investments in capacity creation. The Southern NGOs have opted to continue the data collection and analysis process. It is expected that the information about regional and national resources will become much more widely available through this process, as well as in the deliberations associated with the IWGCB (henceforth referred to as IFCB – the International Forum on Capacity-Building).

Northern NGOs: Deliverers of Capacity-Building

An international committee of Northern NGOs concerned with capacity-building developed a survey questionnaire and a consultation process to assess their views and experience. The committee used these data collection and analysis processes with Northern NGO communities in North America, Europe and Asia-Pacific. The distances involved made consultations across regions impossible, but some consultations did take place within regions. More than 60 Northern NGOs participated in questionnaire surveys or consultations: 36 NGOs from two countries (Canada, the United States) in North America; nine NGOs from seven countries (Denmark, Finland, Ireland, Netherlands, Spain, Sweden and the United Kingdom) in Europe, and 17 NGOs from two countries (Australia, New Zealand) in the Asia-Pacific region. For a variety of reasons the response rate was very low in European countries, so that the results have to be treated as especially tentative for that region. Further information about European and Japanese NGOs was expected to be available at the Brussels conference.

There is little agreement among Northern NGOs about the definition of 'capacity-building' which runs from very specific ('training to implement a programme') to very general ('any activities which increase our partner's abilities ... to improve the lives of the poor'). But the concept is very popular. Nine out of ten Northern NGOs claim to be involved in capacity-building and more than half have a formal policy or programme – a substantial increase over the frequency of programmes identified in past surveys. Training remains the most prevalent approach, though support for networking amongst NGOs and technical assistance are increasingly common forms.

The present priorities of capacity-building programmes offered by Northern NGOs emphasise building the capacities of individuals, such as staff development and leadership development, and enhancing the capabilities of organisations, such as programme design and implementation, organisation development and renewal and planning and strategic management. Most respondents did not describe what they thought made capacity-building programmes effective. Northern NGOs expect future capacity-building programmes to put more emphasis on expanding NGO impacts, such as networking with other NGOs, understanding and influencing policies and monitoring and evaluation to learn from experience.

Northern NGO reasons for co-operating with Southern NGOs stressed increasing the scale and quality of programme outcomes and expanding mutual learning. Like their Southern partners, they were concerned about establishing trust and mutual respect, preserving NGO independence and gaining agreement on development goals and priorities. The report indicates that Northern NGOs are increasingly aware of the importance of supporting Southern NGO efforts to establish and maintain organisational identities and the need to promote more South to South network development.

Although the data collection process focused on capacity-building for Southern NGOs, some Northern NGOs also noted that the positioning of Northern NGOs between donor agencies and Southern NGOs constrained their activities. The report points out that the growing emphasis on capacity-building implies a radical shift in the roles of Northern NGOs, and questions whether Northern NGOs can or should move into capacity-building in place of prior roles (for example, as funders of Southern NGO activities).

Donors: Support for Capacity-Building

The report on donors – foundations, bilateral agencies and multilateral organisations – is based on survey questionnaires answered by respondents in North America, Europe and Asia-Pacific, and on case studies carried out with organisations headquartered in North America and Europe. The donor report is based on much more detailed information than was available for the other stakeholders. Twenty-three donor agencies, including eight foundations, six bilateral agencies and nine multilateral agencies answered an initial questionnaire about their capacity-building activities. Twelve donors participated in extensive interviews and discussions of their roles as well. At least four donor agencies are reported to be undertaking reviews of their own activities in capacity-building with Southern NGOs. The interest in reflection on capacity-building initiatives and impacts visible among Southern NGOs seems to have affected donor agencies as well.

The detailed nature of the information gathered from the group provides a window to donor perspectives on key issues. It is clear, for example, that the different types of donor agencies have different experiences in Southern NGO capacity-building.

Multilateral Agencies

These, for example, have long histories of dealing with governments, but less experience in dealing with Southern NGOs. Many of them are now experimenting with small grants programmes and other initiatives that enable them to deal with civil society actors. It remains a challenge for most multilateral agencies to become 'partners' with what are inevitably much smaller and less bureaucratic organisations.

Bilateral Donors

In contrast, these donors have usually provided support for Southern NGO capacity-building through their national NGO intermediaries. In some cases this has enabled the development of mutually influential partnerships for capacity-building, though Southern NGOs report this outcome less frequently than Northern NGOs. Many bilateral donors have capacity-building experience with government agencies, but that experience has often not been generalised easily to NGOs. Some bilateral donors are now experimenting with capacity-building programmes that serve Southern NGOs directly.

Foundations

Foundations have the most ability and experience in working directly with Southern NGOs and community-based organisations. Some foundations have developed long-term relationships characterised by mutual trust and respect with NGO partners, and have become very sophisticated about the kinds of relationship and assistance required for effective programmes.

The data from donors portrays the current importance of different capacity-building activities and the changes in emphasis experienced over the last five years and anticipated for the next five. Thus cross-sectoral collaboration capacity is currently the most emphasised capacity and the one expected to increase most in the next five years. Monitoring and evaluation and local resource mobilisation are relatively under-emphasised now, but are expected to have the largest increases in emphasis over the next five years. It is quite striking that in this analysis no elements of capacity-building are expected to decrease in emphasis: all will increase or at least remain constant.

The donor report identifies and describes many innovations in capacity-building, including:

- developing strategies for assessing capacity-building needs and assessing programme impacts;
- separating funding from the choice of service and so empowering recipients in their relations with providers;
- reorganising donor requirements to reduce demands on recipients;
- expanding capacity-building support beyond technical assistance and training;

• enabling links to government, business and local foundations.

The report identifies five issues that donors perceive as important for the future:

1. fostering increased capacity and co-operation with Southern NGOs;
2. building a shared definition of capacity-building and assessment of its impacts;
3. identifying and sharing best practices and innovations in capacity-building;
4. improving donor practice to match their rhetoric of partnership and 'demand-driven' capacity-building; and
5. building relationships with Southern NGOs that enable effective negotiations to tailor capacity-building support to meet real needs.

It seems clear from the report that donor agencies expect to increase the resources and energy committed to capacity-building in the future, and that they need to build a better understanding of what works best in different settings. It seems likely that donors will expand the variety of Southern civil society organisations with whom they work to include civil society organisations other than Southern NGOs. In terms of the content of capacity-building, we can expect increasing donor attention to inter-sectoral co-operation amongst civil society, business and government organisations; the problems of financial sustainability and strained relations between NGOs and governments.

PRIORITIES FOR FUTURE CAPACITY-BUILDING

We asked respondents to identify areas of capacity-building that they expected to be important in the future. The results of these questions are summarised in Table 1 by stakeholder group (in the columns) and by capacity-building area (in the rows). In the table, the original list of capacity-building topics has been grouped into four capacity clusters: individual, organisational, resource mobilisation and relations with other actors. These clusters are roughly ordered by the increasing scale of capacity involved.

While the combination of data collection methods used makes it difficult to compare the different groups directly, it is possible to see from these data the relative priorities they assigned to the different kinds of capacity-building for the future. In Table 1.1 we have identified the top ten priorities ('x') in all groups and the top three ('xx') for all but the Southeast Asian NGOs. Preliminary examination of Table 1.1 suggests several areas for further discussion.

Individual Capacities

Leadership development programmes for both existing and 'second-generation' leaders was a matter of interest in several regions, and a top priority in South Asia and Southern and Eastern Africa. Many recognised that NGOs must often move beyond the capacities of charismatic founders if they are to have the wider impact on development contemplated for civil society in many countries. Others saw staff development of various kinds as an important area for future work. The issue of gender sensitivity generated polarised reactions: it was ranked as a high priority area in Southern and Eastern Africa, but dismissed as a 'donor-driven' issue by some other respondents.

In general the issue of individual capacity-building was rated as more important by Southern NGOs than by Northern NGOs or donors. If this is true it may be useful to promote further discussion of issues like the importance of leadership development programmes, the kinds of leadership capacity-building that can be supported by many different stakeholders and the ways in which 'first generation' leaders can help prepare the 'next generation'.

Organisational Capacities

The area of organisational capacity-building was generally given high priority by Southern NGOs. Planning and strategic management was the only area rated as high priority by every SNGO region. Organisation renewal and development and programme design and management were also accorded high priority by most regions. Capacity for monitoring and evaluation was rated as a highest priority by Latin American NGOs as well as by donors and Northern NGOs. Donors and Northern NGOs, however, accorded less importance to other areas of organisational capacity-building.

This divergence of priorities may also be an area to be explored in dialogues among capacity-building stakeholders. Issues that need further exploration include the ways in which donors and Northern NGOs can support the organisational capacity-building deemed as important by Southern NGOs, the delivery of organisational capacity-building through South-to-South programmes and the use of programmes with Northern support (e.g. monitoring and evaluation) to catalyse capacity-building in Southern priority areas (e.g. strategic management, programme design).

Capacity for Resource Mobilisation

SNGOs are understandably concerned about financial resources, and seek capacities for fund-raising and for mobilising local resources. SNGOs in the Horn of Africa voted en masse to emphasise core funding from donors as an essential need – an item not included in the original list of priorities. Donors and Northern NGOs, not surprisingly, are concerned with promoting local resource mobilisation, which will increase the likelihood that programmes will be locally sustainable.

Widespread concern with the sustainability of development services and the shrinking size of international aid resources make this area central to the future of NGOs in many regions. Further discussion is needed to explore issues like the links between capacity-building for resource mobilisation and fund-raising and other kinds of capacity in Southern NGOs, the evolving resource needs of different countries and regions and the emergence of national and sectoral institutions to support the resource needs of Southern NGOs and civil societies.

External Relations Capacities

The issue of Southern NGO capacity for external relations, especially with governments and other civil society actors, was given very high priority by Northern NGOs and donors. Southern NGOs also give high priority to building capacity for policy analysis and advocacy and to networking with other NGOs. On the other hand, the high donor priority for promoting better inter-sectoral relations was only partly reciprocated by SNGOs. SNGOs did not rate collaborating with business as a high priority, except in Latin America. Improving relations with the larger public, with donor agencies and with Northern NGOs was not accorded high priority by SNGOs or by many Northern NGOs or donors.

As Southern NGOs play increasingly significant roles in development, it is probably inevitable that the importance of their relations with external constituencies, from donors to governments to businesses, will increase. Further exploration of issues like the roles of Southern NGOs in development policy-making and implementation, their linkages to business interests and their relations with other civil society organisations is already under way in many settings. These issues have important implications for the development of Southern NGO capacities as well.

Table 1. 1: Future Capacity-Building Priorities for Stakeholders

Capacity (xx = top 3 priorities; x = top 10 priorities)	Southern NGOs					N NGOs	Donors
	South Asia	Southeast Asia	S & E Africa	Horn of Africa	Latin America		
Individual							
Leadership development	xx		xx				x
Staff Development		x		xx	x		
Gender sensitivity		xx				x	x
Organisational							
Planning and strategic management	xx	x	xx	xx	x		x
Organisation renewal and development	x	x			xx	x	x
Project programme design and management	x	x	x	xx		x	
Monitoring and evaluation				x	xx	xx	xx
Financial systems		x		xx			
Information access, storage, dissemination	x		xx			x	x
Research, documenting & perspective-building					x		
Resources							
Fund-raising	x		x		xx		
Local resource mobilisation	x		x	x		x	xx
Core funding for NGO (added item)				xx			
External Relations							
Policy research, analysis and advocacy	xx	x		x	x	xx	x
Networking: other NGOs		x	x	x	x	xx	x*
Networking: civil society organisations		x	x			x	
Networking: Northern NGOs							
Collaboration with government		x	x		x		xx**
Collaboration with business				x		—	
Clarifying NGO roles and identities		x		x			—
Improving governance and accountability		x					—
Strengthening public support						x	—
Improving relations with donor agencies							—

Notes: *   Items combined in the donor questionnaire as 'networking'.
       **   Items combined in the donor questionnaire as 'inter-sectoral collaboration'.
       —   Items not included in the NNGO or donor questionnaire.

Common Themes?

While there are many differences across regions, Southern NGOs seem to agree on some common concerns. There is wide agreement that some organisational capacities, such as planning and strategic management, programme design and management and organisation development, will be increasingly important. There is also wide agreement that some external relations capacities, such as networking and policy influence, will be increasingly important. Northern NGOs and donors agree with the importance accorded to policy influence and networking, and they add monitoring and evaluation and inter-sectoral relations to the list.

But there is not universal agreement on most of these priorities. No 'one size' for capacity-building will 'fit all' SNGOs. Appropriate capacity-building programmes may require extensive negotiation and joint discussion to adapt to local, national and regional needs, and to respond to the concerns of diverse recipients as well as the interests of those who deliver capacity-building services.

BENEFITS AND ISSUES OF NORTH-SOUTH CO-OPERATION

Much past capacity-building for Southern NGOs has been delivered by Northern NGOs, often acting for bilateral donor agencies. Because the relationships between stakeholders in capacity-building programmes are critical to programme outcomes, we also invited Northern and Southern NGO respondents to reflect on the benefits and issues involved in North-South co-operation. Donor respondents were not asked to answer these questions.

Table 1.2 presents the results of these discussions in a format similar to Table 1.1. The columns are organised by regions, and items in the original lists of benefits and issues are grouped into benefits, relationship issues, and programme issues.

Benefits of North-South Co-operation

The most widely recognised benefits of North-South co-operation, from the point of view of Southern NGOs, include enhanced organisation and management capacities and increased programme quality. For both African regions, the availability of financial resources was of the highest importance. Some sub-regions were particularly concerned with opportunities to learn from joint experience or to increase programme scale. The latter two were the top priorities of Northern NGOs. The benefits of co-operation include mutual learning for both Northern and Southern actors, but their other priorities are quite different.

23

Table 1.2: Benefits and Issues in North-South NGO Collaboration

	Southern NGOs					NNGOs
BENEFITS: (xx = one most important; x = three most important)	**South Asia**	**Southeast Asia**	**S & E Africa**	**Horn of Africa**	**Latin America**	
Enhancing organisation and management capacities		X	X	X		
Increasing programme quality	X	X	X			
Making financial resources available (added item)			XX	XX		
Enabling more mutual learning from experience	XX			XX		X
Increasing programme scale or impact	X		X			XX
Increasing legitimacy with other stakeholders						
Promoting more effective advocacy						
ISSUES: (xx = two most important x = five most important)						
A. Relationship Concerns						
Establishing mutual trust and respect	X		XX	XX		XX
Preserving NGO mission and independence			X	XX		XX
Agreement on development goals and values	XX	X				X
Agreement on causes of development problems	XX	X				
Creating mechanisms to resolve conflicts	X					
B. Program Concerns						
Agreement about programme monitoring and evaluation	X			X		X
Agreement about programme design				X		X
Agreement about cost-sharing				X		
Incompatibilities in programmes and operational priorities	X					
Agreement about staff salaries						
Agreement about financial and accounting systems						

Rachel Rowland; Senior Lecturer, Centre for Rural Development

Given the different issues brought to joint ventures by Southern and Northern NGOs, it is important to explore how programmes can be designed to meet the concerns of Northern and Southern stakeholders with diverse agendas. Where financial flows are central to the partnership, it will also be important to explore how parties can avoid one-sided influence patterns that produce dependence rather than effective co-operation, and so undermine rather than encourage self-sustaining development desired by virtually all the stakeholders.

Relationship Concerns

Both Southern and Northern NGOs see relationship issues as more important than programme concerns. Concern with establishing mutual trust and respect is widely recognised as a crucial issue by both Southern and Northern actors. Negotiating agreement on goals, values and problem analysis is particularly important to Asian NGOs, many of whom are concerned about the imposition of models that are culturally and politically inappropriate. African NGOs are particularly concerned with preserving their identities and independence, which are seriously threatened by financial dependence on Northern partners. Indeed, many African NGOs expressed high levels of cynicism about North-South 'partnerships' in consultations: *'we'll do what we have to do to get the money'*, was a comment by many participants.

For many Southern NGOs relationship problems were endemic to their experience with Northern NGOs, and they reported that the establishment of mutual trust and respect was much more difficult than is suggested by the wide-spread agreement among both Northern and Southern NGOs on its importance. It will be essential to explore further the present barriers and facilitators for developing mutual trust and respect, the ways in which Northern NGOs can work with Southern partners without undermining their identities and indepen-dence and effective options for resolving conflicts and repairing relationships.

Programme Concerns

Issues related to the design and implementation of programmes seemed to gen-erate less concern than issues of relationship for both Northern and Southern NGOs. It may be that issues of implementation are an expected and, as more responsibility shifts to Southern NGOs for implementation, a routine part of joint work. These issues are real but manageable – in contrast to relationship problems where the lack of mutual trust or threats to the NGO's independence can create fundamental ruptures in co-operation that are difficult to manage.

But concerns with programme vary considerably across regions. Some regions, such as Southeast Asia or Southern and Eastern Africa, report relative-ly little concern with programme problems, while others, such as the Horn of Africa, report many more concerns.

The data on North-South co-operation, even more than the data on future priorities, suggest that regional differences are important. Relationships between Northern and Southern NGOs are particularly problematic in Africa, where they have been plagued by excessive dependence and power asymmetries. Better understanding of how Northern and Southern actors can work together effectively will need to be worked out in terms of specific regions, countries and relationships rather than dealt with in general abstractions or policies.

ISSUES IN CAPACITY-BUILDING

Discussions in national and regional consultations have raised a number of issues about the processes by which capacity-building is carried out. Whatever the content of priorities negotiated amongst providers and recipients, there are challenges in developing capacities that must be met. The discussion below summarises some important concerns that are already visible.

What is capacity-building and who defines it?

The definition of the capacities needed will shape the programmes designed to build them. Historically capacity-building has often been equated with short-term, individual-centred, content-focused training designed to enhance the capacities of individuals. The discussions summarised here suggest that capacity-building must often be focused on long-term rather than short-term development of capabilities, if it is to have sustainable impacts. It must strengthen the capacities of groups, organisations, networks and sectors as well as individuals if it is to fulfil its promise for widespread impact on development activities. It must catalyse ongoing processes that enable continued learning and growth rather than narrow, content-defined outcomes that encourage one-shot 'fixes'. Training individuals is an important component of capacity-building for Southern NGOs, but it is only one element of what could be a much broader concept that includes a wide variety of interventions that can strengthen Southern NGO roles in development – from team-building with key leadership groups, to organisation design and development consultations, to network building and support programmes, to enhancing legal frameworks and tax policies that foster or inhibit the development of NGOs as a sector.

Recipient response to capacity-building programmes is greatly affected by their perception of its relevance to their own values and goals. When capacity is seen as essential, individuals, groups and organisations often invest much time, energy and talent to build it. The same actors may prove very slow learners if the capacities are perceived to be imposed in response to someone else's agenda.

Different stakeholders see needs for different capacities. If the definition of needed capacities is dominated by Northern actors, capacity-building programme will reflect their perspectives, interests and preferences. Many Southern NGOs see past emphasis on training for accounting and financial management, for example, as a response to Northern concerns with accountability for resources they contribute, rather than as an effort to build capacities needed to implement SNGO missions or to promote sustainable local development.

Northern donors will not surrender all influence over the definition of needed capacities and the means to develop them. But there is much evidence to suggest that capacity-building programmes will produce more sustainable, locally adapted and continually expanding capacities when Southern NGO recipients also shape the definition of those programmes and believe the capacities delivered are important to accomplishing their own development goals. In the Philippines-Canada Human Resource Development Program (PCHRD), for example, programme goals and resource allocations were decided by a joint committee of Canadian and Filipino NGOs. Over a seven year period, the programme made grants to more than a thousand projects and catalysed effective capacity-building initiatives at many levels, enhancing the contributions of individuals, organisations and multi-organisation coalitions. While the Northern donors and NGOs yielded some control of programme decisions, the result has been many high-impact innovations that have built a wide range of local capacities. Mutual influence in the definition and development of capacity-building programmes can integrate the legitimate interests of both Southern NGOs and resource providers.

The challenges of jointly defining and developing capacity-building programmes are substantial, given the range of stakeholders to whom the various parties must be accountable. More exploration of approaches to mutual definition and development of capacity-building initiatives is badly needed.

How can the politics of capacity-building be managed constructively?

The report of the South Asian NGO consultations is titled 'Politics of Capacity-building', reflecting concerns with the problems of power differences, dependency and autonomy that were central issues in many discussions. Indeed, two African consultations largely ignored the issues of North-South co-operation because of widespread belief that their concerns would not have any impact. The dominant sentiment for many African NGOs was characterised as: 'It's useless to talk about these issues. Just tell us what we have to do to get the money'.

If capacity-building initiatives embody and reinforce Northern dominance and Southern dependence or punish instances of Southern NGO autonomy and initiative, programme impacts in terms of capacity-building and sustainability are likely to be counter-productive. It is easy for donors, seen by recipients as very powerful in their ability to control essential resources, to remain unaware of how much communications can be distorted by real or perceived power asymmetries. Potential beneficiaries of capacity-building programmes may be reluctant to explain what kinds of programme are really needed for fear they will be perceived as unworthy of future support. It may be necessary to explicitly design programmes to protect recipients from perceived risks of being honest about their deficiencies or challenging donor assumptions and behaviour that creates problems. For example, the Ford Foundation was concerned about such risks in offering organisational capacity-building services to its grass-roots grantees in the United States. The Foundation subsidised consulting assistance with the explicit understanding that the consultation would not be shared with the Foundation, so grantees did not have to worry about the consequences of frank discussions of their shortcomings with the consultants. Under these conditions, many grantees made constructive use of the services.

Power differences are inevitable among stakeholders in many capacity-building programmes. But the perverse effects of those differences and politics that undermine the creation of relevant and sustainable capacities can be better understood and managed if the stakeholders recognise potential problems and define programmes to deal with them.

How can capacity-building be contextualised to fit local circumstances?

Many discussions focused on past experience with capacity-building as a 'supply-driven' service offered by outside actors, rather than a 'demand-driven' service oriented to the concerns and priorities of recipients. Many capacity-building programmes are rooted in experience and are implemented by organisations and staff that are distant from the experience of Southern NGOs. To become effective and appropriate to local circumstances, programmes may have to be extensively 'contextualised' to fit the cultural expectations, political contexts, economic circumstances and historical development of Southern civil societies and NGO communities. More specifically, capacity-building initiatives may have to be tailored to the identities and strategies, programmatic focus and stages of development of individual NGOs.

Even when programmes are initially tailored to fit local needs, the capacity to continuously redesign and adapt capacity-building initiatives becomes critically important when NGOs are operating in contexts that are undergoing rapid political, economic and social change. Regional and national support organisations that can help catalyse the transformation of capacity-building initiatives to fit evolving circumstances may become increasingly central. For example, the regional NGO support organisation MWENGO (The Eastern and Southern African NGO Reflection and Development Centre) has linked with national NGO associations and outside resources to create workshops on issues such as NGO identity and strategic thinking, policy advocacy and fund-raising. These programmes provide opportunities to adapt experience and frameworks from many countries and regions to fit local concerns, while the central role of national associations ensures relevance and accountability to their Southern NGO members.

The challenges of contextualising capacity-building to fit a wide range of local circumstances are very complex. It is not always clear that Southern NGOs know what they need, in part because civil societies face rapidly evolving challenges and very diverse circumstances and they often have little access to information about useful capacities. But much can be done to create strategies for diagnosing the needs that are emerging and customising available training, consulting and capacity-building technologies to fit those needs.

How can productive capacity-building relationships be constructed?

Establishing mutual trust and respect was seen as essential to productive capacity-building relationships by many respondents, both Northern and Southern. The top priority issues for North-South co-operation were relationship problems rather than programme matters. Building productive relationships may be particularly difficult when Northern and Southern actors are separated by huge differences in perceived wealth, power and resources. When such differences are perceived, as in the case of many African NGOs, problems of trust, respect and dependence may dominate the relationship even when the parties have good intentions. For NGOs with more diversified access to resources, such as many Asian NGOs, the relationship difficulties may focus on negotiating shared values, goals and diagnoses of development problems.

Creating productive capacity-building relations may be facilitated by long-term commitment to joint work that serves the interests and utilises the comparative advantages of all the parties. Such relations require all participants to recognise the special contributions available from each member, and their interdependence for achieving desired goals. It is difficult to develop mutual influence unless Northerners recognise the resources brought by Southern partners (e.g. access to grass-roots populations, creative local development initiatives) as well as Southerners recognising the resources brought by Northerners (e.g. technical skills, resources for programme expansion). For example, the Global Partnership for NGO Studies, Education and Training has developed mutually supporting training programmes for NGO activists in Asia, Africa and North America. The partners – BRAC (Bangladesh Rural Advancement Committee), ORAP (Organisation of Rural Associations for Progress, Zimbabwe) and SIT

(School for International Training, USA) – built an alliance on the strengths of their existing programmes that increases the educational resources available to their students as well as expanding the student bodies available to all of them.

How can the capacity of communities of NGOs – NGO sectors – be enhanced?

Many national and regional communities of Southern NGOs have become increasingly aware of the need for enhancing the capacity of groups of NGOs that share national, regional or issue-based concerns. Enhanced abilities to share information, articulate shared policy positions, or initiate collective action on matters of joint interest can be of great value, especially in interacting with other actors – such as governments, businesses, and donors – that customarily operate at levels of aggregation larger than most Southern NGOs. An association of NGOs with common interests, such as the National NGO Council of Kenya, or the Association of Development Agencies of Bangladesh, can represent NGO interests in discussions with donors or governments in ways not feasible to single NGOs. Support for capacity-building for such associations may enable a sectoral voice in national affairs that would otherwise remain unheard,

Southern NGO communities may also be strengthened by supporting the emergence of national or local support organisations that provide relevant capacity-building assistance to the Southern NGO sector. Such support organisations can multiply the impacts of successful programmes by translating them into local languages, circumstances and cultures in ways that would be very difficult for Northern actors. The Society for Participatory Research in Asia (PRIA), for example, has built a network of autonomous support organisations to provide participatory research, human resource development, organisation development and policy analysis and advocacy support to Southern NGOs all over India. The resulting network offers programmes in languages and regions well beyond what was possible to the parent organisation.

Participants in many consultations pointed out that there is enormous, largely untapped, potential for South-to-South capacity-building relationships. Such partnerships may quickly overcome many of the credibility problems that plague North-to-South programmes, since Southern actors often understand from personal experience the problems faced by their colleagues. Solutions grounded in Southern experience may also have more credibility than tools that emerge from Northern experience. Sectoral strengths in some countries or regions could be used to catalyse enhanced capacities in less favoured areas. For example, the Latin American network for capacity-building, FICONG, surveyed capacity-building in Latin America and identified many regional organisations and programmes that offered needed resources. Much of the capacity-building in that region may be carried out by Southern actors, grounded in regional expertise.

But such relationships are often hampered by the lack of resources that Northern NGOs and donors may be able to mobilise. We need to understand fully how to develop relationships that make good use of the special resources of both Southern and Northern actors in capacity-building initiatives to strengthen the sector as a whole.

How should capacity-building be monitored and evaluated?

The challenge of monitoring and evaluating development programmes in general is drawing increasing attention as many actors become more concerned with learning from experience and assessing impacts of their programmes. Monitoring and evaluating capacity-building initiatives presents special challenges, since improvement in many important capacities (e.g. strategic management, organisation renewal, policy advocacy) is not easy to measure. The current concern among many resource providers with measurable 'results' risks focusing attention on easily-measured outcomes (e.g. quality of accounts, loan repayment rates) at the expense of difficult-to-measure (e.g. growth in entrepreneurial initiatives), but critically important, aspects of capacity development.

Traditional external evaluation approaches to assessing impacts are currently being supplemented with a wide variety of participatory methods that stress enhancing the capacities of the evaluated programme or institution as well as obtaining solid information about is performance.

The problem of developing participatory monitoring and evaluation processes that enable the parties to exert mutual influence on the results and their interpretation is receiving increasing attention. A recent conference sponsored by the Institute for Development Studies at the University of Sussex and the International Institute for Rural Reconstruction in Manila brought together participants in dozens of such efforts to begin identifying the critical elements of successful joint learning. The World Bank has also begun publishing materials and holding workshops for participatory monitoring and evaluation. There is increasing experience with strategies and tools for joint reflection and learning that can be used to supplement as well as assess capacity-building initiatives.

In assessing capacity-building a first step may be to mobilise the recipients to articulate their own goals, describe their progress and assess how their goals are advanced (or retarded) by their experiences. The national and regional initiatives to continue discussions of capacity-building priorities by NGOs in Asia and Latin America may be a critical step toward monitoring and evaluating future efforts. Similarly initiatives currently under way to reflect on experience with capacity-building and to develop participatory monitoring and evaluation initiatives may also shed more light on these issues.

DISCUSSION: FUTURE SNGO CAPACITY-BUILDING

The surveys and consultations with Southern NGOs, Northern NGOs and donors indicated widespread agreement on the need for future capacity-building in areas such as planning and strategic management, organisation renewal and development, project design and management, policy research and advocacy and network building with other NGOs. Other areas were seen as critical to some regions and not to others (e.g. leadership development in South Asia, Southern and Eastern Africa; gender sensitivity in Southern and Eastern Africa, financial systems and core funding in the Horn of Africa). Some areas were high priorities for Southern NGOs and not for Northern NGOs or donors (e.g. leadership development); others were high priority for Northern NGOs and donors but not for many Southern NGOs (e.g. gender sensitivity, inter-sectoral collaboration).

It is possible to identify general topics for capacity-building initiatives, but the relevance of those initiatives to specific regions and countries should be negotiated on a case-by-case basis. Global offerings of 'supply-driven' programmes will be much less useful than programmes that are 'demand-driven' by locally recognised needs.

The data suggest that Northern and Southern NGOs see the benefits of co-operation quite differently: Northern NGOs emphasise increased programme scale and mutual learning, and Southern NGOs emphasise increased programme quality, organisational capacity, and financial resources as well as mutual learning. Southern and Northern NGOs agree on the importance of relationship concerns in co-operation. To the extent that Northern NGOs are themselves constrained by their place in the institutional chain of development – for example subject to the policies and regulations of bilateral donors – they may not always be free to negotiate the co-operative relationships and structures they might prefer in relations with Southern NGOs. But the ways in which capacity-building is defined and delivered may still be critical to its sustainability and utilisation.

There has been virtually no question amongst the participants in these surveys and consultations about the importance of capacity-building – there is widespread agreement that sustainable improvements in the lives of millions depend on improving the capacities of civil society actors. What requires attention is the development of strategies, programmes and relationships for building those capacities.

Part Two

Capacity-Building of Individual Organisations

Chapter 2

Capacity-Building through Leadership Development: The African Churches Experience

Margaret W. Mwaura
CORAT AFRICA

In the past capacity-building has been viewed as synonymous with training. The almost exclusive emphasis on technical training has been broadened to encompass more management and organisational issues. Training itself is no longer seen as the only way to build NGO capacity. Training does still remain, however, the single most common approach to capacity-building. Training tends to focus on capacity-building of individuals to take back their learning to then influence organisational capacity-building.

CORAT(Christian Organisations Research Advisory Trust) has over 25 years of providing training to churches and NGOs in Africa. During this time they have learnt a great deal about what makes for effective training in Africa. In this chapter they show how the external changes in the environment have firstly called the churches to leadership in their country's development, but that this calling requires the church to demonstrate effective leadership within its own structures. Leadership development is seen as a critical capacity-building intervention for churches to fulfil their role in development.

THE CALL *TO* LEADERSHIP: THE CHALLENGES FACING THE CHURCH IN AFRICA

As the new millennium begins, Africa as a continent is experiencing severe challenges in the economic, social and political spheres. The church in Africa does not have the option of being able to sit on the sideline and observe and comment on such issues. It is being called on to provide moral and spiritual leadership in addressing these challenges.

Poverty is a major challenge in many African countries with most of the populace living below the poverty line. In Tanzania for instance 85% of population and in Sudan 90% of the population live below the poverty line. Some of the manifestations of poverty are lack of housing, inadequate health facilities, hunger, problems of unemployment and underemployment, lack of access to education and malnutrition. The church has sometimes been accused of being too silent about oppression of the poor in our society, but increasingly the church is recognising the impact on itself when people (including its members) cannot meet their basic needs of survival.

The rising incidences of **HIV/AIDS** disease is also associated with poverty and requires leaders who can cope with and provide leadership to meet the needs. Resources are crucial for helping and caring for the orphans and families affected by the disease. Sometimes churches have been overwhelmed by the demands associated with HIV/AIDS. In most African countries the problem of street children continues to challenge policy-makers as well as church leaders. It seems that the more programs that are initiated to address the problem the more children are on the streets.

The church has been involved in advocacy on **human rights** issues. In many African countries the tension between the church and state has always been of concern and sometimes the church has been seen by the government as supporting the opposition. For the church to be effective in providing leadership, it needs the capacity to confront the government with documented evidence and materials that are convincing. This, therefore means that the church should be able and well equipped for the daunting task. The church ought to be seen as a defender of the weak and the vulnerable in the society.

The population growth and demands on the land result in unemployment which leads to **migration** to urban areas in search of employment. This further leads to a number of social problems and strain on the infrastructure in the urban areas. The problems posed by this phenomenon also affect the churches as they face a membership that has diverse needs, especially in the urban areas. Church leaders need to be properly equipped to cope with problems and challenges posed by rural/urban migration.

The **cultural and moral values** have and continue to be eroded especially due to the effect of so-called modernisation and Westernisation. This has affected the family and hence the society sometimes negatively. According to Dr Hannah Kinoti:

Yet there is no denying that in spite of these discernible moral values, which are still very much part of the rural majority and to some extent African estates in urban areas, moral decay is evident everywhere. This is one of the many contradictions and paradoxes of Africa today. I suggest that part of the process of reconstruction is the need for the church to take stock of her historical, structural, theological and cultural contribution to the moral state of affairs in Africa today. Then because the church is still divinely mandated with moral authority, she should continue giving leadership in a more forthright manner'[5]

THE CALL FOR LEADERSHIP: THE NEED FOR LEADERSHIP IN CHURCHES

In order to provide Africa with moral and spiritual leadership in responding to these severe **external** challenges, churches themselves need to be strong and in particular have high quality leaders. As well as being strong enough to respond to the considerable external challenges in the environment, the church needs leaders capable of acting on the many **internal challenges** the church itself is facing.

Some of the major internal challenges for churches to address are issues of their:

- role,
- vision,
- governance,
- culture, and
- change.

In terms of role, church leadership should be both professional and spiritual in nature. Church leaders though trained in theology are assigned responsibilities which go beyond the teaching of theology. If one is assigned to co-ordinate development, health work or to manage an institution, theological training will be of little help. There is usually a tension within churches between the 'secular' and the 'spiritual' which manifests itself in a number of ways. Sometimes it is revealed by attention not being paid to recruiting qualified staff or by ignoring the volunteer potential of highly qualified professionals who are church members.

It is evident that churches need a **clear vision** of how they might address the severe challenges facing them. In the past the churches had been more reactive, appearing to address the problems which others, like donors, were willing to finance. Hence, churches found themselves in a very vulnerable position. The church leadership needs to be strengthened to clearly determine their vision, priorities and strategies. Donor partners involved in capacity-building ought to desist from giving directives and allow for participation in identifying the pri-

[5] H. Kinoti 'The Church in the Reconstruction of our Moral Self' in J.N.K. Mugambi (ed.) The Church and Reconstruction of Africa

orities for the churches in social development and capacity-building. The church leadership ought, therefore, to have a clear vision and sound strategy and also be in a position to utilise the skills and talents of its available human and financial resources.

The **boards and committees**, which are expected to provide the guidance and leadership in most church institutions, tend to be very weak. They are not well informed of their roles and responsibilities. Though it is dangerous to generalise, the poor performance by the board and committees often results from the way they are constituted. In some cases board members are chosen because of their position in the church (e.g. clergy, staff, etc.) without considering their ability to make significant contribution. Where constitutions do not exist the leader usually decides how and who is invited to the board or the committee. It is imperative to establish a system of developing, training and renewing the board to ensure that its members are adequately equipped with the knowledge, skills and attitudes to undertake their responsibilities. Any meaningful leadership development needs to address this issue.

It is also important to understand the **organisational/church culture** as it influences leadership and capacity-building. From CORAT's experience of working with churches, there are a number of common cultural issues which churches may need to identify and then address. These may include:

A culture of <u>dependence</u>: In many mainline churches, the majority of funds are not self-generated from tithes and offerings, but given by international donors. This has resulted in a culture of dependence whereby churches wait for initiative and help from outside and/or do not question any donor-initiated changes in strategy. The culture becomes reactive and passive.

A culture of <u>conflict avoidance/obedience</u>: Many church cultures avoid conflict which must be faced. Some churches retain staff without the resources to pay them instead of retrenching. While avoiding the painful issues of retrenchment in the short-term, the long-term issues will not simply disappear and morale will continue to go down until eventually something is done. It takes courage on the part of the leadership to face up to the realities of the day.

A culture of <u>loyalty/obedience</u>. In other cases, any conflict with the leadership is avoided and their actions not questioned (even when they are clearly wrong). For example, it is not uncommon for staff to be aware of (and constrained by) their boundaries. They may be bound by church regulations to be loyal to the bishop and his very powerful procurator. This culture of loyalty can block any attempt to bring basic and necessary changes.

These common internal challenges of churches are currently made even more acute by the need for churches themselves to be 'led' through necessary change processes as they **adapt to their changing environment**. The mainstream churches in Africa are experiencing 'turbulent times' at the moment. With funds from international donors shrinking rapidly, the churches have become aware of the need to have professional, effective leaders who are adaptable (and able to adapt their churches) to the changing environment.

The church in Africa is generally viewed as 'poor'. As a result finances to run churches have usually been provided by donors in the North. Available local resources have not been fully exploited. With current challenges of globalisation resulting in dwindling resources for financing church activities, churches have been forced to rethink their future sustainability. The churches which were established by Mission Boards are the hardest hit. The new upcoming Charismatic churches, without such connections, survive on the members' donations and yet their membership tends not to be the well-to-do in society. This has made most people start re-evaluating their dependency status. What is evident is that the churches should impress upon their members the need to support their churches. In the process of challenging members to change, the leadership faces resistance because members are not used to giving to meet the churches need. This has, in some cases, resulted in mistrust of the local leaders who have taken up leadership positions subsequent to missionaries from the West returning to their countries. Managing change and the challenges that go with change are issues that must be addressed in developing leadership.

Strong, visionary and humble leaders are critical if churches are to address their internal challenges and to provide the moral and spiritual leadership to address the massive external challenges of poverty.

The need for leadership development

Church leaders must be properly equipped to manage and meet the many responsibilities placed upon them. There are, however, only limited attempts to consciously develop the necessary leadership. It is assumed that having attended seminaries or bible school clerics are able to direct complex and large organisations. The preparation most church leaders receive during their training does not usually provide them with skills necessary to perform the leadership tasks of providing direction, policy and strategy for the church.

This lack of leadership development continues to impact on other issues relating to the church such as human and material resources. Leadership development for the church should be geared towards bridging the skills gap that has existed in the church in Africa for a long time.

DEVELOPING LEADERSHIP

The Christian Organisations Research and Advisory Trust (CORAT) was established in 1975 to enable churches and church-related organisations to improve their management capability. CORAT started in recognition of the critical need for better management and leadership in Christian organisations, seasoned by scriptures, African cultural insights and the best in management. CORAT uses a biblical model of 'servant leadership' as Jesus the master teacher came to serve and not to be served (this contrasts with common practice in Africa where leadership has been portrayed as power that lords itself over everyone else). CORAT's services to churches are also influenced by an understanding of leaders as 'stewards'. The leader is expected to be a steward of the available resources and be accountable to God and the people. In an environment where corruption is rampant as in Africa, the church leader is expected to provide the necessary leadership in the area of combating corruption.

CORAT provides training, consultancy and research services to develop leadership, organisation and management within churches throughout Africa from its base in Kenya.

Training
Pan African Residential Training
CORAT has organised residential courses since 1981. Participants, drawn from different denominations and countries, are brought together for training relevant to their work, such as *financial management, management for development workers, senior church administrators*. The training offers participants opportunities not only to learn management skills of planning, organising, controlling and communication, but also develop character through such topics as integrity, stewardship and accountability. The acquiring of values of change of heart is as important as the development of skills.

In all cases, the facilitators use a biblical approach to ensure that training is as tailored to the participants' cultural context as possible. The bible contains considerable management and leadership principles. The training also provides the participants with opportunities to share and learn from one another.

The duration of the courses ranges from two to ten weeks. The assessment of the impact shows that some participants have been able to implement the training with great success. Some have been promoted to top leadership positions and others have influenced change by inviting CORAT to provide in-house training and long-term accompaniment assignments.

The strengths of this type of training is in participants being equipped with specific skills, knowledge and attitude for better performance. Open training also enables the exchange of information and ideas from different countries and churches. Residential courses allow concentration on the matter in hand.

The main weakness, which has been evident and acknowledged, is that the participants return to institutions that are operating under the same culture as before. Hence it is difficult for one individual to change others who have not received the same training.

To address this challenge, two to three participants from each organisation are invited to attend the courses and they usually prepare an action plan on an area where they will implement learning. Together with facilitators and other participants, they identify forces that may hinder and forces that may help their implementation. With the introduction of action plans, reports show that a number of participants have succeeded in introducing change.

In-House Tailor-Made Courses

CORAT has also been involved in organising tailor-made courses for church personnel. Such courses may be a result of an evaluation or training needs assessment. In a number of cases, CORAT has had the opportunity to train all the clergy or the development workers of a given diocese.

CORAT delivers an average of twenty courses in a year throughout Africa. These courses are intended to address the weaknesses of training one individual in isolation who is unable to implement the training on returning. The training targets members of staff in one organisation and the content of the course is discussed and agreed with the client to ensure that it meets the specific needs of the organisations. These types of courses have been seen to be more cost effective and the churches are finding it possible to make a contribution and meet the greater part of the cost.

While training, particularly in-house training, has strengthened the capacity of personnel, this sometimes does not translate into more effective organisations. In many instances people have recommended quick solutions only to discover that even those solutions do not perform the miracles anticipated. For training to be effective it is necessary to assess not only the skill, knowledge and attitude deficiencies, but also the organisational issues that should be addressed to provide a conducive environment for change. Among the factors that determine the effectiveness of training are: commitment of the leadership, participants and conducive environments for teamwork and appreciation by leadership for good management and accountability. In fact it is the commitment of the church leadership that is the primordial factor determining effectiveness of such training. Their motivation to change plays a major role.

Training Top Leadership

In 1998, a unique training programme for bishops, administrators and co-ordinators was organised. The assumption was that the leaders lack the knowledge, skills and attitude needed for transformational leadership and therefore, the chance and opportunity for learning. The programme 'Future Leadership' was developed and aimed at:

- building and strengthening the skills of the top leaders of the church, and also changing attitudes. Organisational change rarely takes place if the leader is not committed;
- enhancing the knowledge and skills in leadership and management for the leading group of the church institution;
- transforming the leaders into transformational leadership teams;
- implanting the message of their own responsibility for change; and
- equipping these teams with some basic skills to start organisational change processes in their institution.

Approach
The course took cognisance of the fact that church leaders are very busy and therefore adjusted the approach to their tight schedules. Instead of a one long period, the programme was divided into four parts (referred to as modules) of three days each. Past experience has shown that leaders attended courses alone which was not very effective. This particular course was targeted at the top leadership, which included the bishop, the administrator and co-ordinator. These are the core people in the church structure. The groups would met separately, though covering the same topics for free and in-depth discussions. Thereafter the three groups met and deliberated on their dilemmas together.

This approach had three major advantages:

- The church leaders who would otherwise have been too busy to attend a workshop were able to leave their stations for short periods four times in the year.
- In between the modules, the participants were able to put their learning into practice and share their challenges in the next module.
- It provided an opportunity for the groups to meet with their peers in private and also to share in one forum (which is not very usual in the church structure).

Topics Covered
This course was developed in recognition of the need for more professional, effective and adaptive leadership to the changing environment in which the church is operating. With this in mind, the following topics were covered in the various modules:

- Self-awareness
- Understanding /diagnosing organisational culture
- Leadership styles
- Managing conflicts
- Effective communication
- Problem-solving
- The learning organisation
- Power and leadership
- Coaching as a leadership tool
- Management of change
- Vision building

Results to Date

At the end of the course, participants were asked to create their own action plans. These included organising seminars to share the learnings from the future leadership course. To date feedback has been received from a number of the participants stating progress on the their achievements and there are a number of reports of improved working relationships.

Given that CORAT charges full-cost recovery fees for its services, a measure of the perceived value of the capacity-building services by the clients is the level of repeat business.

- Dioceses that were represented in the course have nominated their staff to relevant courses at CORAT.
- CORAT has been asked to conduct seminars for some dioceses.
- A number of letters have requested CORAT to collaborate with the dioceses in certain areas of their work.
- The course has generated Organisation Development (OD) consultancy work for CORAT.

Organisation Development

As well as the traditional training courses, CORAT provides Organisation Development (OD) consultancy services to churches. Organisational Development is an approach that is gaining popularity in church circles and it is hoped that it will help them address some of their organisational problems. The emphasis is on taking the organisation through a process of change that is planned and owned by the stakeholders. Due to the culture of dependency on donor funding, the tendency is sometimes to feel overwhelmed by the changing realities. The need to reflect on the past in order to shape the future becomes more and more important. Reflecting on the past enables churches both to identify landmark/milestones that build a momentum for the desired future and to point out pitfalls to avoid in order to move towards a better future.

Many organisations and donors are now turning to organisational development. The approach is long term and focuses not only on the efficiency, effectiveness, achievements and impact but also on the organisational culture, relationship, human resources development. Of course as long as the initiative and ownership remains with the donor it is likely to face a problem. Where the process is, however, owned by the client it can have far-reaching positive results on the organisation and its sustainability. Experience with churches, however, shows that the process is too expensive for them and, hence, in most cases the donors have provided financial support (though care is taken to ensure that ownership remains with the client).

Capacity-building is ultimately dependent on people. Whatever approach or strategy is used for capacity-building, it is the human factor which determines its success or its failure. Human beings are the ones to decide what is important and then influence the process.

Chapter 3

Key Success Factors in Capacity-Building: Lessons from OD Consultancy Experience

Rick James
INTRAC

The CORAT case illustrated the need to put individual-focused capacity-building interventions into an organisational context. As a result, CORAT has shifted from merely providing open training to in-house training and to offering OD consultancy services too. OD consultancy is a potentially effective approach to NGO capacity-building because it focuses on organisations; recognising their complexity and emphasising the importance of core organisation issues. It also stresses the importance of being able to adapt to the changing environment.

Like capacity-building, OD is another much abused term. OD consultancy is not synonymous with capacity-building, but is one specific type of capacity-building intervention. This chapter attempts to clarify understanding of the term and outline the key factors for its success. It is clear that these key success factors are not limited merely to OD, but are very applicable to other capacity-building interventions.

INTRODUCTION

Organisation Development (OD) consultancy is being seen as a key approach to NGO capacity-building. OD is currently being prioritised as a key development strategy by a number of major European NGOs such as Novib, Hivos, CORDAID, Oxfam, Norwegian Church Aid, and Danchurchaid. A recent survey of Northern[6] NGO approaches to capacity-building of Southern[7] NGOs revealed

---

[6] Throughout this publication, Northern NGOs will be used to refer to NGOs from the OECD countries (recognising that this division is far from geographically accurate).
[7] Southern NGOs correspond to NGOs from traditional aid-recipient countries

that 'Organisation Development and Renewal' is currently the main capacity-building priority for Northern NGOs (James et al. 1998). As with capacity-building itself, OD tends to be defined very vaguely if at all. Another piece of research with European NGOs concluded, 'few agencies were either really clear what they meant by OD or had developed policies and strategies for OD (with one or two notable exceptions)'. Even one of the most experienced agencies with OD admitted, 'we have not defined it yet as an organisation and we use the term very loosely' (James, 1998: 14)

This chapter aims to define what is meant by OD consultancy and describe what such a capacity-building intervention looks like in practice. The chapter will then go on to highlight some of the key success factors of OD consultancy which emerged out of an 18-month research project examining nine cases of actual OD interventions with NGOs in six African countries (for more detailed information see James, R., 1998, 'Demystifying Organisation Development: Practical Capacity-Building Experiences of African NGOs,' INTRAC). The key success factors highlighted have important implications for other capacity-building interventions as well as for donors and Northern NGOs wishing to support such initiatives.

TOWARDS A DEFINITION OF OD – TEN CORE INGREDIENTS OF OD

While there is a diversity of approaches to and definitions of OD, some core elements in OD do exist and can form the basis of a workable definition. The following common elements of OD represent a set of ideals or ingredients. In reality every situation will be different and not all OD interventions will have the same emphasis (or amount) of each ingredient. What is important, however, that there is at least a flavour of each ingredient in the OD intervention.

1. The goal of OD is not just that an organisation can solve its current problem today, but that it can be strengthened to solve its future problems too

OD stresses developing client capabilities for future problem-solving. Most change efforts focus on solving existing problems in an organisation. Although this is one goal of OD, what distinguishes OD from other change efforts is its emphasis on developing clients' capabilities for problem-solving after the consultant has gone. According to Schein, 'it is a critical assumption ... that problems will stay solved longer and be solved more effectively if the organisation solves those problems itself' (1988:7).

45

2. OD helps organisations become more able to 'learn'

Integrally related to being able to solve its future problems is the position that a key product of an OD intervention is that an NGO becomes more of a 'learning organisation'. It is argued that, in the present climate, change is so rapid that all you can do is develop capacity within an organisation to adapt to change: 'learning how to learn continuously and consciously from lived experience is the key if we are to avoid being overtaken and overwhelmed by environmental change' (Revens quoted in Blunt and Jones 1992:213). Becoming a 'learning organisation' is at the heart of OD and is one of the crucial tests of the effectiveness of an OD intervention. As Alan Fowler expresses it, 'if an OD process goes well, it never stops, but becomes a way of life' (1997:192).

3. OD sees organisations as whole systems of interrelated components, working with groups not just individuals

OD views organisations from a systems perspectives where issues, events and forces within organisations are not isolated but interrelated. Organisations are viewed holistically whereby a change in any one part of an organisation has an impact on the rest of the organisation. As Campbell states:

> All four (structure, staff, strategy, teams) have to be brought together in one strategy designed to improve the effectiveness of the organisation. This is what OD is all about: helping the NGO look at all aspects of the organisation in a coherent and comprehensive way. (1994: vi)

Furthermore OD is a process of people learning to change together not apart. The focus is on the development of groups and organisations. Individual development is promoted only when it is required to improve group functioning.

4. OD focuses on organisational culture

In recent years the importance of an organisation's 'culture' in determining how it functions has been increasingly emphasised. Culture can be defined as a 'pattern of learned underlying assumptions about how to behave' or in more colloquial language 'the way we do things round here'. Organisations are much more complex than the formal aspects which can be easily seen 'above the water-line' such as the organisational charts, the job descriptions, the mission statements or strategic plans. The ways in which organisations perform are often influenced more by the informal actions which occur 'below the water-line' such as the way people relate unofficially, the political manoeuvring, the personalities involved, the ways decisions are made.

The analogy of a hippo or an iceberg is often used to illustrate this reality. In more literary terms, Schein likens culture to lily pads:

> There you can see the lilies floating on top of the pond ... but you do not see the roots that may go down 10–15 feet, deeply bedded down in the mud that made the lily pad grow. If you do not get down into these roots and down into the mud, you do not understand the whole process'.(Schein quoted in Info-line 1988:5)

OD stresses the centrality of culture to organisational change. Burke (1987) states that one of the three criteria for deciding whether an intervention can be classified as OD is whether it brings about a change in organisational culture. This is on the premise that 'the overarching determinant of how organisations work is the culture that is evolved in the organisation' (Schein quoted in Blunt 1995:213). The poor performance of most top-down corporate culture change programmes, however, has led to recent emphasis that 'rather than trying to manage culture though culture change programmes, you should consider your cultural context whenever you contemplate or carry out organisational change' (Hatch 1997:235).

It is also increasingly recognised in OD that politics and vested interests form a very considerable part of the informal organisation. The OD gospel of openness, trust and authenticity is losing some of its political naiveté and developing greater awareness of the sources of power within the organisation and how they must be recognised and used to bring about change.

5. OD is about conscious, not accidental, change

Organisations develop, change and grow irrespective of any intervention. There are inherent life processes which occur naturally. OD, or perhaps more accurately OD interventions, are conscious attempts to help organisations become more effective in their work and adaptive to their environment. This conscious approach to change shows that 'while change is inevitable, change that *happens* to an organisation can be distinguished from change that is *planned* by organisational members' (Huse and Cummings 1985:19). In the past OD has been defined as a process of *planned* change in which the nature of the change is defined and owned by the organisation. Controls and levers, such as indicators and planning tools, are increasingly popular in encouraging organisational change but it has been questioned whether change can really be controlled and planned – the idea of OD as a conscious attempt to foster change is seen as more realistic.

6. OD encompasses a process of collaborative diagnosis based on action research

It is difficult to overstate the importance of diagnosis in the change process in determining the priority issues; the type of intervention needed; whether there is sufficient internal commitment to change. As Albrecht says, 'prescription without diagnosis is malpractice whether in medicine or management' (quoted in Info-Line 1988:7). This diagnosis should be a process of self-appraisal by the client (often facilitated), not expert, external appraisal where the consultant does the diagnosis.

OD is based on an action research model of continual data collection, analysis and feedback for collective awareness - on the assumption that for effective change to occur, issues and solutions should be owned internally not displaced. This is underpinned by a normative, re-educative change strategy 'which works with the heart and the head by supporting learning processes that accept the psychological resistance to the change of fundamental attitudes' (Rao and Kellerher 1995:3).

7. OD focuses on people, not physical resources

The emphasis of OD is on human resources, their motivation, utilisation and integration within the organisation and is therefore NOT about purchasing new equipment, raising money or redesigning the project. Organisations are seen to be composed of a collection of human beings interacting together. Change in peoples' behaviour is a major concern and therefore collaboration is stressed not only as a useful process, but also as a key outcome.

8. OD uses both micro-and increasingly macro-activities

OD uses a variety of planned programmatic activities designed to help an organisation become more effective. Recently there has been an increasing shift from process-related micro-interventions such as group dynamics, work design, leadership, to more performance-related macro-activities focusing on strategy, structure and relations to environment reflecting senior executive interest in task issues rather than relationship issues.

There is widening recognition of the need to take into account the external environment in diagnosing the health of an organisation, especially as the NGO environment is being seen as increasingly chaotic.

9. OD has an ongoing process nature

Because we live in a state of continuous change and because addressing issues of culture may involve long-standing deeply engrained patterns of behaviour, OD is not a one-shot solution. It is a long-term, systemic process striving towards greater effectiveness through a series of interventions over time. Some distinguish authentic OD on the length of interventions and say that a little OD may even be a dangerous thing as 'small amounts of OD training may serve to surface problems, but do not allow for sufficient time to let the staff deal constructively and thoroughly with problems' (Fullan et al. quoted in Walters 1990:215).

OD tends to be differentiated from other forms of organisational consultancy in the way it is done, rather than necessarily the content alone. For example, a strategic planning exercise may be done in an outside prescriptive way leaving the organisation as incapacitated as before, and therefore share little in common with principles of OD, whereas another strategic planning exercise may be facilitated in such a way as to be entirely consistent with these principles. Our definition of ODC is different from prescriptive and problem-solving management consultancy – sometimes known as the 'mafia model' whereby an outside expert comes in and tells the client of the problems and the solutions.

10. OD focuses on improving the organisational effectiveness as defined by the organisation itself

OD must meet a felt need of the organisation and have an end of improved performance, not be an end in itself.

THE DIFFERENT TECHNIQUES, TOOLS AND METHODS WHICH ODC USES

Some of the problems which arise from confusion and a lack of definitions of OD can be addressed by understanding more about what sorts of intervention are being discussed when the term OD is used. One way of analysing OD interventions is by classifying them according to where the focus of the intervention is: on the individual; the team; intergroup relations or on the whole organisation.

Major Families Of OD Interventions

Individual	Team	Intergroup Relations	Total Organisation
Life and career planning	Team-building Conflict resolution	Intergroup activities Conflict resolution	Strategic management, planning, visioning
Coaching and counselling	Survey feedback	Survey feedback	Survey feedback
Education and training	Process consultation	Process consultation	Technostructural change
Stress management	HRM systems	Strategic planning activities	Culture change
			HRM systems development

Shifts in OD   Most recently

There have been recent shifts in the practice of OD from a focus on interventions primarily directed inside the organisation such as group process, behavioural activities, to interventions which treat outward elements, such as strategy and task. This reflects the increasing recognition of the importance of the external environment in organisational effectiveness. At the same time there has been a broadening of OD interventions from an almost exclusive focus on teams and intergroup relations to include interventions which deal either with the whole organisation or which recognise the critical role of individuals in top leadership positions. As can be clearly seen in the typology, some interventions affect more than one area.

LOMADEF – Case Study by Joyce Kezesi Mataya (CABUNGO)

In 1993 a dynamic Malawian community leader, Mr J. J. Kanjanga, returned from a church-sponsored training programme in organic farming and sustainable development practice. He was so inspired by a vision to pass on his learnings to assist his community that LOMADEF (Lipangwe Organic Manure Demonstration Farm) was born. During the next five years LOMADEF slowly established seven farmers clubs centred around Mr Kanjanga's demonstration plot. Here people would learn sustainable development practices which they were encouraged to replicate on their own land.

In an effort to scale-up the impact of LOMADEF, Mr Kanjanga approached an international NGO for funding, and while this was one of the INGO's priority funding areas, they were concerned that LOMADEF lacked a clear picture of how it would develop over the coming years. It seemed highly dependent on one individual.

This funder approached CABUNGO, a Malawian NGO provider of OD services, to see if they could assist, and CABUNGO made it clear that LOMADEF had to own the need for the OD services and therefore had to make the request direct to CABUNGO. After tripartite meetings between the various stakeholders, which clarified misunderstandings LOMADEF approached CABUNGO directly for help to address some of the organisational challenges it was facing.

A participative organisational assessment process took place in order to develop a common understanding of where LOMADEF has come from, how it is performing, how healthy is it in terms of relationships, communication and shared ideas and how it relates to the wider environment. The assessment took place over several days with interviews between CABUNGO OD practitioners and a variety of LOMADEF stakeholders. The assessment culminated in a three-day workshop to discuss and analyse the findings. The LOMADEF stakeholders highlighted major challenges of:

- a lack of shared ownership and decision-making (everything rested with the founder);
- a lack of clearly understood purpose and strategy which led to the organisation trying to respond to unlimited community needs;
- a lack of land ownership – the demonstration plot was on Mr Kanjanga's own land which was causing some misunderstandings; and
- an unclear relationship between LOMADEF and the church which had originally financed the training.

In order to address some of these challenges CABUNGO, the OD provider:

1. facilitated a workshop for LOMADEF to develop a clear vision, mission and strategy;
2. facilitated a workshop for club chairpersons and members of a newly formed executive committee to look at leadership issues and practices;
3. supplied financial management training for committee members and club treasurers to help them develop appropriate book-keeping and accounting systems; and
4. is providing support in developing appropriate systems, procedures and job descriptions.

What is the difference in LOMADEF before and after the OD intervention?

- It has set up an executive committee which shares management and decision-making. There is much wider 'ownership' of LOMADEF by its members.
- It has a mission statement and defined strategy to guide activities and prevent it becoming overstretched during the next few years.
- This mission and strategy have been shared by all clubs through an awareness and publicity campaign in their areas.
- The clubs and main demonstration plot have been allocated land by the local chiefs.
- The number of clubs have grown from 7 to 36, each with about 18 members.
- LOMADEF has secured funding from the INGO for the next three years as well as from a bilateral donor

These achievements, particularly the securing of relatively large funding, have also brought their own challenges in turn. An organisation cannot afford to relax, but has to continually change and adapt to the new challenges it faces.

KEY SUCCESS FACTORS IN OD CONSULTANCY

The INTRAC research into the practice of OD with African NGOs highlighted certain key success factors which can be usefully analysed through this simple model:

The Context

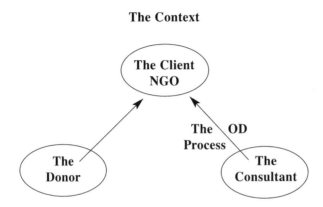

The Context

The wider context in which the NGO operates has a very considerable and often under-rated influence on the capacity-building process. As Bebbington and Mitlin point out, 'NGOs and capacity-building are highly vulnerable to the general context in which they are working' (1996: 25). The research corroborated these statements as it was often changes in the wider environment, such as political change in South Africa or Namibia or donor changes in Europe which were the triggers and external pressures which forced NGOs to change and adapt to a new reality.

The context of South Africa, for example, obviously had a massive impact on the practice of OD consultancy. The end of apartheid created a massive need for NGOs to radically rethink their whole identity and role in development (and therefore undertake OD processes). This need was accentuated by many NGOs having traditional funding relationships threatened and in some cases broken. At the same time, the desire to contribute to the 'new South Africa' meant that donors were much more open to funding OD processes than in other countries. In addition, OD in South Africa benefited from a history of questioning, and a desire for change. One client also described how, '*the changes in South Africa made us more self-assured of our existence and relevance than before. It made us more free, reflective and self-critical*'. South Africa had the other advantages of a high education level and a ready supply of OD consultants – many of whom might be described as white liberals who did not think it was right to run NGOs themselves, but who wanted to contribute to these NGOs being effective.

Similarly, in Eritrea the recent political climate was also conducive to OD. With 'independence', all institutions were questioning how they could contribute most effectively to the new society. The Eritrean case had the added advantage in their OD process of being supported by the government and society at large. This translated into significant financial support which freed the NGO from having to respond to donor demands.

Conversely, in other countries the context has had a less 'favourable' influence on the impact of the OD interventions. For example, the case from Namibia showed that years of poor education for black Namibians made the need for OD with the NGO much greater, but at the same time it meant that *'the OD process will take longer and be more expensive'*. With other cases from Malawi, Kenya and Tanzania, it was clear that environmental factors such as the level of literacy and the topography, climate and road systems in the region all served to slow down the OD process and would have slowed down any other capacity-building intervention. The more difficult the context, therefore, the greater the capacity-building need, but also the more constraints on capacity-building interventions.

The Client NGO
Ownership
The prime factor determining the success or otherwise of an OD intervention mentioned by almost every respondent throughout the research was that the **NGO itself owned the change process**. NGOs had to have a felt need for change and be prepared to make their own investment of considerable time, effort and resources in the process. The cases demonstrate this clearly, with many of them paying for workshop costs and consultant fees themselves. In the words of one client, *'we paid for it ourselves initially ... if you do not do it yourself, you do not take it as seriously'*. There were also considerable non-financial costs which clients had to bear: *'little did we know how tough it is. It is taking a massive amount of time and extra effort and frustration on our part with a high personal cost on our children'*. As an example of this commitment, one respondent from this organisation voluntarily travelled 210 km just to be interviewed in the research.

The ownership of the change process is closely related to how keenly the NGO perceives the need. Unless key people in the organisation feel the need for change none is likely to occur. Some NGOs believed the situation to be so desperate that they had no choice and so the onus on change was high.

Conditions need to exist which preclude the maintenance of the status quo. For organisations really to take on the tensions and effort of change and overcome the inherent resistances it must be clear that not changing would be even more dangerous and threatening. In many cases consultants use 'future scenario' tools to reveal the massive cost of doing nothing. Kotter states that for a change process to succeed 75% of management must be honestly convinced that business as usual is unacceptable (1995:62). Respondents thought that it was necessary to have a sense of urgency with the organisation 'in pain, but not too much pain' – facing a **'moderate' crisis**! If the crisis, however, was too acute, then more immediate (and coercive) approaches might be more appropriate. Two of the OD cases, however, were with NGOs at points of relative stability rather than crisis. While the change process may have been owned as much by these two organisations, perhaps the extent of their actual change was less.

The cases did reveal the value of having both **internal and external pressures for change**. Internal pressures for change were important to ensure peoples' commitment as shown by NGO's recognition of their own weaknesses and dissatisfaction with their current performance. These internal pressures are often articulated in staff beliefs that they are constantly fire-fighting; overstretched; and unable to meet beneficiary demands; and are seen in low staff morale and increasing staff turnover.

While these internal pressures are essential, more frequently the required 'crisis' is actually triggered by external factors such as negative donor evaluations and 'doubts over resources'. The moment the funding future is less secure, then suddenly NGOs become more open to change. Some respondents even thought that *'funding insecurity is a precondition for change'*! If there are already sufficient internal pressures for change (a felt need) then it does not seem to be a problem that external factors trigger the change process. This external trigger can be likened to a match which will be effective in lighting a fire only if kindling is already there. If there are no such internal pressures, the match will burn brightly, but quickly fizzle and die.

The level of ownership of a change programme is closely correlated with the **nature of leadership support**. While some change initiatives might have emanated from the staff, unless the leadership supported these change efforts or came to support them, it appeared they were doomed to fail. Almost all the cases described the critical role of leadership in driving the change process. Leadership acceptance is not enough – their positive energies are essential for its success. As one of the consultants in the case studies reported,

> The organisation did shift, the conflict was resolved – in part because leadership made unbelievable changes – and the entire strategy changed ... leaders often have to go through the most major changes, which often means letting go of past perceptions which is

difficult. If leadership can't shift, then no organisational process can succeed. (Kaplan 1995:2)

Leaders must have an understanding of the need for change, the emotional acceptance of that change and the will to implement it in their organisations and with themselves. The leadership must also have ownership of the process, not just the need for change. The case studies also reveal that ownership and top management commitment are not static phenomena. In some examples, leadership commitment was not really there at the start, but it was the process itself that brought this with leaders mentioning 'a moment of truth' for the leadership well into the OD process – the will of the organisation sometimes needs to be awoken.

Staff Involvement and Ownership
There also needs to be individual ability and willingness of staff throughout the organisation to make changes. Organisational change is as much a political or social process as it is technical. **A critical mass of support** is therefore necessary with key change agents at different points in the organisation. Powerful coalitions need to be formed with enough power within the organisation to manage the change process. Identifying key opinion leaders (or 'will' carriers) is a common and effective part of many approaches to change. One of the main factors in the success of one of the cases was the existence of key change agents within the programme as well as having the full-time commitment of a powerful staff member. In another example the organisation had the advantage that the staff were ex-combatants and had extremely strong team spirit. They were used to working together. They had been sharing their beliefs, pain and dreams for many years.

Ultimately the effectiveness of the actual implementation of any change will largely depend on how the staff view the changes. If key stakeholders are not involved little will change in practice, which is why for effective change one consultant said '*you need a culture of openness which should be built in from the start*' – the nature of the intervention process itself therefore was seen as crucial.

The OD Intervention Process
As well as ensuring that the need for change is clearly owned by the organisation, the cases indicate that design and implementation of the intervention process itself had an impact on the effectiveness of the work.

The principles of good practice in implementing OD processes which emerge from the cases are that they need to be **participatory**. To ensure staff ownership of the change process, their involvement in the intervention was seen as vital. The examples all demonstrated participative processes (though to differing degrees and at different points). In one example, it was said that *'staff were involved throughout the process'*, and others commented on how the participative workshops had *'built trust and recognition'*. The participative workshop aspect of the OD interventions was seen as critical in enhancing staff ownership of both the needs and the solutions.

The OD processes needed to be given **enough time**. Again and again, the importance of allowing the process sufficient time was noted by clients, consultants and even some donors: *'we need to slow the pace of change down because to get real depth and quality you need time'*. People were aware of the danger that *'we are always in such a hurry to see results that we spoil the process'*. The successful cases reveal an incremental approach which starts from where people are and goes at a pace which can be coped with *'at peoples' own pace'*, as otherwise *'it is very draining to do too much organisational change too quickly'*. Kotter puts it clearly when he says that 'the change process goes through a series of phases that in total usually require a considerable length of time. Skipping steps creates only the illusion of speed' (Kotter 1995).

Closely related to allowing the process sufficient time was the need to develop a **flexible and an intermittent process**. One consultant described OD as *'an unfolding process where you cannot know everything at the beginning. You have to start outside and work towards the heart'*. Some of the successful interventions were flexible, integrated processes which occurred at periodic moments over a number of years.

The cases also illustrate the OD principle of assessing the **whole organisation** and seeing the interrelated elements, including the board. One of the cases illustrated the problem that when the director and chair of the board left, there remained other board members who had not been part of the process. Another church-related case showed how it is important for church-based organisations to overcome the dualistic pastoral/development division and to work with the whole organisation to effect meaningful change.

OD processes benefited from understanding the political dimensions of organisations. Organisations are intensely political entities – to facilitate change effectively the **political 'power points'** need to be identified and appropriate strategies developed.

The OD interventions in the cases were thought to be more effective if there was sufficient **follow-through**, and the need for this should be discussed at the initial stage of contracting for the consultancy to ensure that both the client and the consultant allow enough time for this.

Clear plans with indicators and bench-marks also strengthened the OD interventions where definite time schedules with roles and responsibilities were allocated. One of the case study clients noted *'we have set plans and goals to* *implement changes'*. There needs to be constant monitoring of the change process, as well as designing it to allow for 'short-term wins' (some quick, visible results to motivate staff further).

The cases also showed the benefit of using a **variety of change strategies**. Training was used as a key complement to consultancy in many of the cases.

The Consultants

The nature of the OD process designed obviously is inextricably linked with the person designing it. The critical importance of the skills, knowledge and attitudes of the consultants emerged clearly from the cases.

Consultants had to **quickly build a relationship of confidence and trust** with the NGO if the intervention was to work. This obviously helps if consultants have worked with clients over a period time and can help if clients have the impression that, as one client said, *'he knows us better than we know our own pockets'*.

Consultants also employed **appropriate consulting styles** and had well-developed personal skills to lead clients through very sensitive and at times conflictive processes. One case showed how different 'confrontational and acceptant' consulting styles were used to great effect in such circumstances. Another consultant was described by the client as having a *'very people-friendly style'* and that he was *'the best person who has ever worked with us in all the time I have been here'*.

The case studies revealed the importance of consultants having **well-developed communication skills**. They benefited from good verbal communication skills in the mother tongue of the client group. The problem of having translators was mentioned in some cases even though the facilitators were Africans. Conversely with another case, the client noted that the consultant was able to *'speak the language of the people, not just the development office'*. Yet language ability alone is not enough as *'effective communication required a profound interpretation of cultural imagery and metaphor'* according to one consultant. The importance of good written communication skills was also obvious from the cases. One client stated that *'the reports of Olive were very helpful. They were thorough and accessible with prompt clear recommendations and conclusions'*.

Consultants also needed to have an analytical ability, experience and insight to **understand the reality of the client**, especially the local NGO context and values. While it was felt this might be easier if the consultant was from the same country, *'as it is easy for foreigners to misunderstand behaviour and cultural cues'* this was clearly not a sufficient condition. One example showed the advantages of having local external consultants with insight and experience hold up a 'critical mirror' of the prevailing culture of the organisation.

As well as knowing the local NGO context, the OD consultant needed to have a good sense of the **wider picture**, to see how the world is changing and how this might affect the NGO concerned. The benefit of having someone on the consultancy team who understood the perspective of the Northern NGO donors was often mentioned.

The cases also revealed the importance of the **consultants' attitude and approach** in giving inputs in such a way that the process of OD can be guided from within. One client responded that *'we were surprised by their approach which made us think for ourselves and so what we came out with was ours not theirs. We expected them to assist us to get what we want to do, instead they have guided us to think what we want to do'*. Others mentioned the importance of the consultants challenging them, saying, *'they kept reminding us that we could not abdicate responsibility. They kept putting us back in the driving seat'* and sometimes even said to them, *'I wonder if you will really do this. This must be your decision otherwise nothing will change'*.

Good consultants have to be **clear about their briefs, roles and boundaries**. One case demonstrated the need to analyse regularly the roles the consultants played and renegotiate them as appropriate. As the client said, *'Olive has been very careful to get a clear sense of their brief and been very sensitive in checking back. I do not feel either organisation exceeded its mandate. Both (Olive and CDRA) were very thorough and cautious about the brief and if anything underplay their role to ensure our ownership'*.

The **availability of the consultants** was a very real issue. While one client commented, *'every time I had a problem his doors were open. I frequently stopped him in the centre of town as he was driving along'* another lamented that, *'they do not have enough time for us ... they are difficult to get hold of'* and feared being left in mid-air.

The Northern NGO Role

The existing relationship between the donor and the NGO also had a very real impact on the success or otherwise of the intervention. There is a danger that OD is driven by well-meaning donors, but 'there is a huge difference between working with clients who really want it and those who have it forced upon them'. As Mosi Kisare has highlighted, *'much of the criticism of OD by NGOs was influenced by a context in which certain conditions are imposed by the North on the South'*, and goes on to point out that sometimes 'those who attempt to impose OD ... are misusing and abusing the discipline of OD for the sake of the imposition of their agenda' (1996:4). He warns of the danger of OD becoming another basis for conditionality and unwarranted intrusion into the affairs of African NGOs, noting that when a donor's project-driven needs are linked to an OD process then it certainly becomes an external agenda and cannot be successful in promoting the organisation development of NGOs (which is why so many external evaluations of NGOs contribute so little to important change processes).

The cases show that an obvious, but critical factor in this relationship is whether the Northern NGOs are prepared **to fund the OD process from a distance**. OD consultancy is expensive and not very 'donor appealing', but those agencies which had been able to access support for their OD greatly appreciated the role the donor had played in supporting the process financially. There is also a need for donors to be prepared to see these processes through and not withdraw support for the OD process when the quick-fix does not materialise. It was believed by Southern respondents that for OD to be effective, Northern NGOs had to stand alongside partners at difficult and 'unattractive' times *'accepting failures as long as it had an overall positive trend'* and accepting slow change. OD needs adequate resources to support and maintain the change which is why it is such a poor 'exit strategy'.

As well as funding, the cases show that the Northern NGO donors also had an important role in **putting OD on the agenda** in the first place. One client responded *'someone has to trigger the idea. Usually it will come from the outside. Often money is involved as money makes people think'*. Another described a positive dialogue with their donor in which *'the idea (for OD) originated from the donor, but was then taken up by the diocese'* and yet another stated that they would not even have started without the assistance of the donor.

The dilemma is how to trigger the process and then stand back and let the process move on its own.

In one of the cases, the donor lost its way a bit and tried to push and direct the process too much: *'deadlines were fixed by the donor which put us under great pressure which was not compatible with the participative process we wanted and the size and poor communications in the diocese. The donor ignored our involvement in pastoral activities'*. Donors can impose arbitrary time limits which do not take into account the local context or the nature of organisational change. Some donors even can be tempted to direct the change process themselves, as in one of the cases, by trying to force the organisation to fire a staff member through making it a funding condition. For consultants, *'it is very difficult to operate as the agent of the funder. People feel coerced and do not see the need themselves'*. The result is that *'OD is less successful in Africa because it is perceived as a Northern donor agenda'*. OD may become so linked to resources that it becomes another required funding hoop and not an approach to strengthen the organisation. Just as consultants have to determine clearly 'who is the client', so too do donors. There is a tendency for Northern donors to identify capacity-building needs in terms of what directly affects them: monitoring and evaluation; financial systems; proposal and report writing. In this case, whose needs is capacity-building primarily serving? Yet it was seen in the cases that donors should not be isolated from the OD process either as *'if they had been more involved in the process they would understand it better and be more supportive of what is going on'*. More significantly, NGOs do not operate in a vacuum, but as part of an open aid system. Donors may well be both a part of the problem and a part of the solution. OD processes which excluded a critical review of the relationships with Northern NGOs were seen as compartmentalising and superficial. Yet this involvement must be appropriate. In one example the donor did not participate in early workshops as it would have been very tempting for the donor to move the process too quickly. At subsequent workshops they were able to be a bit more involved as the organisation was beginning to establish its identity. They could offer their views more constructively once the NGO's confidence had been gained.

SOME IMPLICATIONS FOR NORTHERN NGOS IN SUPPORTING CAPACITY-BUILDING

The investigation of OD consultancy leads to important conclusions for effective Northern NGOs, not just for OD consultancy, but more generally for capacity-building.

Ensure that Ownership of the Change Process is and Remains with the Client

If ownership of the change process is the prerequisite for authentic organisational change, then it is essential for a donor organisation to let the partner lead the process. In this way, it is the partner NGO that must take the lead throughout the decision-making process. While the Northern NGO may have been instrumental in putting capacity-building on the agenda, ownership for the capacity-building process must quickly reside in the client NGO. The Southern partner must be allowed to identify the needs; set the agenda; write the terms of reference and have responsibility for selecting and contracting the support. As EASUN states, *'the issue may be introduced by the donor, paid for by the donor, but still the NGO has to ask us'* otherwise the client may abdicate responsibility for change. While it is fine for a Northern NGO to ask questions and explore ideas, it can be a very thin line between that and organisational manipulation. Part of accepting that the process belongs to another organisation is for the Northern NGO to accept the confidentiality of the process and not demand to see internal reports of the process.

How committed an agency is to let the Southern partner lead the capacity-building process can often be demonstrated by how clearly the real client is defined. The client must be the organisation itself and there should be no possible perception that the change process is for the benefit of the donor. The boundary between the client, the capacity-building body and the donor needs to be carefully managed, so that the capacity-builder can be trusted without being associated with a hidden agenda or seen as agents of the donors. This clarity needs to be reflected in the Terms of Reference and contract where the client organisation is responsible for the hiring (and, if necessary, firing) of the consultant, rather than an arrangement between donor and consultant. Clarifying mutual expectations between consultant and client is an important part of the contract negotiation. The reality in many donor-funded interventions is that donors add a further complication by asking the consultant to report back to them on the client organisation. This undermines the neutrality of the consultant and may well serve to derail the capacity-building intervention.

If the donor does play a role in initiating the change process, it can have deep implications on how organisational change is implemented and whether ownership is really with the client or mere acquiescence. Given their control of key resources, donors run the risk of being perceived as imposing or pressuring change. What appears to a European desk officer as an innocent suggestion can be taken as a donor directive by the local organisation.

Signpost Appropriately

The process of organisational change and development is a complex one which often benefits from the use of external, skilled, experienced consultants or trainers who can provide objectivity and balance without being linked to a funding agenda. The choice of capacity-builder is therefore key. It is vital to find 'good' ones – for OD consultancy the primary success factors in terms of the consultants themselves are exacting but essential as outlined earlier. Sometimes no capacity-building intervention is preferable to a bad one.

There are some areas of capacity-building, such as systems and staff skills, that are not generally very sensitive and it may be appropriate for donors to recommend or employ their own consultants if this is agreed by the partner. There are, however, many issues of capacity-building involving identity, mission and strategy which are much more sensitive and yet donors tend to be blind to the differences. They still recommend or employ their consultants for these areas too, oblivious of the manipulation and controlling messages this sends and the undermining tensions it gives rise to from the start. It is important to create a separate space for organisations to change.

Let the Process Take its own Course

There is a very real danger with most capacity-building programmes that donors will try and force the pace as they are under pressure from their own donors to show concrete results. As Robert Chambers pointed out 'the harvesting cycles of donors and of Third World farmers are fundamentally different' (quoted in Morgan and Qualman 1996:14). Neither OD nor other capacity-building interventions are quick-fix solutions. The cases clearly showed that if in-depth change is desired, it should be allowed to occur at its own pace, rather than by an artificial deadline set by another organisation in another continent. Hastening this process is likely to undermine local ownership and severely reduce the effectiveness of the intervention.

See the Process Through

Capacity-building is a very complex process. It often involves long-term intermittent support which can be costly in time and money – it is not a quick-fix. This has implications for the nature and length of donor support. If the donor supports a capacity-building process, it should be prepared to see it through and not bail out half-way leaving the 'partner' stranded. Obviously it is not possible for donors to guarantee support for the final outcome of a change process, but once they have helped set a process in motion donors should be aware of their responsibilities to see it through.

Co-ordinate with Other Donors

Another important role for Northern NGOs in supporting capacity-building effectively is to ensure that there is co-operation amongst themselves. A capacity-building process can very easily be undermined by another donor who does not share the same understanding of capacity-building or its role in the process. Different donor policies and approaches may well confuse the process. As a result one European NGO, for example, sees an important role of theirs in an OD process to be 'parallel dialogue with other stakeholders (such as World Council of Churches) and ensuring co-operation amongst Aprodev members, particularly Nordics' (James 1998).

Be Part of the Process

Donors have the tendency to compartmentalise capacity-building and limit it to the Southern partner without recognising the important role that the donors themselves play in the 'open' aid delivery system. For a more effective performance of the Southern NGO changes may be required in its relationship with and the behaviour of donors. Donors can ask consultants to fix a recipient's relationship with its own clients, when in fact the problem lies with the donor's relationship with the recipient. Some Northern NGOs, for example, when discussing how to engage in OD with partners rapidly concluded that their own capacity weaknesses have to be recognised and admitted to first, as did their historical role in shaping partners' own capacity.

The building of capacity must be marked by shifts in the partner relationship and so exclusion of the partnership itself from the OD process may be extremely narrow and limiting – though it requires a degree of self-assurance and openness from Northern NGOs which is not always evident. As one Southern NGO notes 'the resources which support the activities of development practitioners come from the powerful and are seldom if ever consciously given with the intention of setting processes in motion that will significantly redress the power differentials against the interests of the donor' (CDRA 1996/7:18).

Remove Your Own Plank – Build Your Own Capacity

If Northern NGOs believe in the effectiveness of capacity-building or OD for 'partners', they should practice it in their own organisations, not just encourage others to use it. There is something very disturbing and inconsistent if organisations only advocate a particular approach with those over whom they have power.

If Northern NGOs do apply OD to themselves they will not only have greater credibility in suggesting it to their partners in the South, but can also put it on the agenda of their own back donors. Perhaps this is the one of the greatest contributions Northern NGOs can make to development – influencing their own back donors.

Part Three

Capacity-Building by Partnerships
Between Organisations

Chapter 4

Case Study of a North-South Partnership: An Analysis of the Capacity-Building Process Between CDS, Cairo and CRDT, UK

Rachel J. Roland[8] and Rasha Omar

Capacity-building programmes are often conceived as something one organisation or individual does to another. They tend to be based on the assumption that the North has much to teach the South. This chapter examines two examples of 'mutual capacity-building' and whether the learning was conceived as two-way from the start at least by the key players if not the donor initially. Two-way capacity-building through non-funding linkages of like-minded organisations in the North and the South offer a very interesting approach to capacity-building. Relations between such organisations, unpolluted by the inherent power dynamics which arise through control over resources tend to be more equal and offer greater opportunities for learning both in the South and the North.

This first example describes a linkage between an Egyptian development agency and a British university which focused on gender.

INTRODUCTION

Strengthening civil society is premised upon creating a space for dialogue, reflection and sharing in decision-making between many different types of organisation. It is a pluralistic process that is enriched by the cross-fertilisation between formal and non-formal, private and public, insider and outsider organisations.

[8] Rachel Roland; Senior Lecturer, Centre for Rural Development and Training (CRDT), University of Wolverhampton, Gorway Road, Walsall, WS1 3BD. Web Address: www.wlv.ac.uk.crdt. E-mail: r.j.roland@wlv.ac.uk Services Management Unit Y, Centre for Development Services (CDS), 4 Sahmed Pasha St,. 6th Floor, Citibank Building, Garden City, CAIRO, Egypt. Web Address: www.nearest.org. E-mail: cd

In a similar vein, partnerships between Northern and Southern organisations are often seen as a means of building the capacity of the Southern NGOs and hence, strengthening civil society in the South. An issue this raises is therefore to what extent is it given that building the capacity of an NGO will automatically strengthen civil society? The debate is wide but this chapter concentrates on the role that North/South partnerships can play in both the internal development of both organisations and in their ability to be effective as actors helping to strengthen civil society in the South and the North.

The partnership between the Center for Development Services (CDS), Cairo and the Centre for Rural Development and Training (CRDT) of the University of Wolverhampton provides an opportunity for reflection and learning. The partnership was born through a funded scheme, from 1992 to 1998 (referred to as the Link) that was focused on gender sensitive development.

This chapter sets out the history and character of the partnership between the organisations and analyses some important aspects related to internal organisational development and how the organisations interact with local communities. The final section will summarise the issues that need to be built upon in future North/South partnerships.

BACKGROUND TO THE LINK SCHEME

The Link

The way that the partnership was established proved influential in its development. The British Council initiated the funding of the partnership through its Higher Education Link Scheme. The objectives of this scheme were to 'promote development and co-operation' between Northern and Southern academic institutions and to strengthen Southern institutions through:

- staff development opportunities;
- course and curriculum development;
- research collaboration;
- management strengthening (British Council 1996).

Therefore the apparent purpose of the Link seemed to be to transfer knowledge and skills from a Northern institution (perceived by the funder as strong) to a Southern organisation (perceived as needing to build its capacity). Although the Link Scheme seemed to target primarily formal education organisations, it also welcomed the participation of non-formal adult education organisations like CRDT and CDS. So it was through this support that the two organisations had the opportunity to enrol in the Link.

The profile of the partner institutions was unique. Although CRDT is a university sector institution, CDS is a non-governmental organisation (NGO). Both deliver human resource development, project management and research services to the public sector, voluntary and private organisations. CRDT operates worldwide and CDS, in Egypt and the Middle East. Both CDS and CRDT are self-financing, not-for-profit organisations.

Another unique feature is that both organisations use learner-centred methods in the delivery of their services instead of the predominating teaching centred approach that is based on behaviourism and transfer of knowledge. Furthermore, the subject matter of the Link and hence the partnership was also unique: it addressed the complex concept of Women in Development and later on, Gender and Development.

Following agreement by the British Council, the Link between CRDT and CDS was set up in April 1992 with the wider aims of:

- increasing awareness of staff concerning the ways in which gender issues can be incorporated into CDS national project activities;
- improving the WID expertise of CDS staff in order to meet the needs of government and other development agencies;
- developing a resource base for WID materials which can be sold or hired to outside bodies for use in National or International WID programmes (British Council, 1992).

The Memorandum of Understanding was renewed twice further. The character of the Link changed with development trends from Women in Development (WID), through Gender and Development (GAD), to gender-sensitive sectoral approaches and most recently to mainstreaming gender in training, consultancy and all aspects of the project cycle. As it ended the Link aims were simply: 'to work with both women and men in order to improve equality of opportunity and equity, specifically focusing on women, (British Council, 1996). The emphasis was on using joint knowledge, skills and attitudes to be effective practitioners in both the organisations and in the work they do.

Benefits of the Link Scheme to CDS and CRDT

Since its establishment in 1990, CDS' mission has been to support people and organisations to realise their full potential and foster self-determined, self-sustaining change. All its training, technical assistance, research or consultancy activities are based on the belief that participation is imperative for learning and change. Early on in CDS, there was an interest to learn about WID and GAD in order to develop its capabilities to address issues of equity of opportunities and resource distribution between women and men. The Link offered that opportunity. The fact that CRDT, had been working in Egypt since 1977, predisposed it to be the partner institution.

Indeed, CRDT had much in common with CDS as well as having the experience of the Egyptian context necessary to be able to contribute to building CDS knowledge, skills and attitudes in the fields of WID and GAD. In particular, CRDT had over 25 years of experience in activities similar to those that CDS was beginning to be involved in, and had for many years worked with participatory approaches to adult and vocational training and education. For CRDT the Link represented an opportunity to deepen understanding of gender training practice, to increase the effectiveness of future work as well as being an opportunity for staff development.

CDS' and CRDT's common characteristics and expectations from the Link inclined both partners to a constructive co-operation. The nature of their activities and the similarity of their approaches led them to opt for training as a means for co-operation. Indeed training was first used to build the capability of CDS staff in WID and GAD. Training was also used to address gender issues in the Egyptian and Middle Eastern communities and with other development practitioners. Table 4.1 illustrates the various training activities implemented throughout the partnership period from 1992 to 1998.

Table 4.1: Activities of the Higher Education Link

DATE	LOCATION	ACTIVITY
May 1992	Egypt	Gender Awareness Workshop run jointly by CDS/CRDT
August 1992	Egypt	Gender Awareness Workshop run jointly by CDS/CRDT
November 1992	Egypt	CRDT Librarian to CDS to help develop library resources in CDS
December 1992	Egypt	Gender Awareness Workshops x 2 run by CDS with support from CRDT
April-June 1993	UK	CDS WID Co-ordinator + Librarian participated in 12-week Women's trainer training at CRDT
1993	Egypt	Publication of first edition of Women's Newsletter
1993	Egypt	Women's Club reopened, with a library.
1994/5	UK	CDS staff member participated in 13-month MSc Development Training and Education at CRDT
1995	UK	CDS staff member participated in 12-week Women's trainer training a at CRDT
1995	Egypt, Jordan and Sudan	3 x Regional Workshops sponsored by the British Council and the Near East Foundation on Gender and Development Programmes in the Arab World. One work shop delivered by CDS and CRDT. Two workshops delivered by CDS and the Near East Foundation in Sudan and Jordan.
October 1996	Cairo	Improving organisational effectiveness from a gender perspective; workshop, with grass-roots organisations in a suburb of Cairo. Workshop jointly designed by CDS and CRDT, delivered by CDS.
June – July 1997	Egypt, UK	Finalisation of a joint concept paper on developing a customised capacity-building programme to strengthen the effectiveness of Egyptian NGOs.
February 1998	Egypt and UK	Joint finalisation of two papers presenting the CDS and CRDT partnership experience.

INTERNAL DEVELOPMENT OF CDS AND CRDT

Examining who was involved in the partnership

Between 1992 and 1999, there have been four CRDT and three CDS co-ordinators managing the teams, working on partnership activities, maintaining relations with the donor, and overseeing logistical and administrative matters pertaining to the partnership. Apart from the co-ordinators, a large number of other staff have also been involved. Over 20 people have worked directly in Link activity teams.

Teamwork was the main way of carrying out activities during the Link. The teams have comprised support and technical staff from a great range of disciplines at different times: from librarianship to health, through agriculture and organisation and management. This reflects the diversity of activities undertaken by both institutions, the multifaceted skills and knowledge of the CDS and CRDT staff and the potential for mainstreaming gender in their work both together and separately.

Women and men have both been involved in the partnership. Working in teams and changing co-ordinators emphasised the learning and staff development aspects of the Link. One of the spin-offs of the teamwork was that it constantly generated new ideas for training programmes that CDS and CRDT could work on, that addressed perceived needs for the development of Egyptian NGO programmes and management skills.

The ease with which the Link operated was due to several factors about the way each organisation already worked. The relative autonomy given to the North/South activity teams by the managers of the organisation meant that ownership of the activities was positive and creative. The teamworking experience each brought to the Link from their own organisation helped in that new attitudes and habits for working together already existed and relations were always adult and cordial. The team's consequent participation in both planning and delivery of the activities meant that individuals followed through on their inputs and there were no mid-activity 'drop-outs'.

CDS capacity-building: learning through experience

When the Link began, CRDT's main role was training CDS staff to enable them to develop the necessary knowledge and skills to deliver and manage gender training programmes. The training took place either on the job or through the participation of selected CDS staff in gender-related courses facilitated by CRDT. CDS was an active seeker of knowledge, learning and using the knowledge and skills gained to explore gender issues from the Egyptian and Middle Eastern perspective, and to produce relevant learning materials. Within the first few years, a cadre of staff was competent to design, deliver and evaluate gender training.

Throughout this process of building knowledge, skills and attitudes, the key elements were the joint reflection and joint planning activities carried out by CDS and CRDT members. The resulting new practice in each iteration of the cycle constituted a new phase in the development of the partnership, as shown in Figure 4.1.

Figure 4.1: Learning through Experience in the Partnership

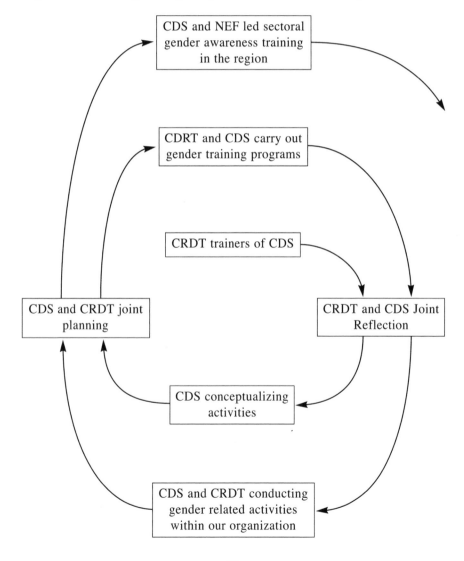

Experiential learning and understanding of the challenges and constraints facing the NGO community in the Arab world enabled the role of CDS to evolve from co-trainers, to lead designers and trainers. The outputs of the partnership that are pertinent to the internal growth and learning of CDS and CRDT are shown in Table 4.2. By working and learning together, each partner has added in a rich sense, to the know-how and 'being' of the other.

This learning through experience approach was key to develop the staff capacities in CDS and CRDT. Both partners realised that they still had a long way to go to fully comprehend the complexities of gender issues in development.

The factors contributing to the success of the learning approach are that:

• A learner-centred approach is embedded in CDS and CRDT's practices. The partnership was an extension of those practices and hence incorporated the same methods of work.
• The availability in both organisations, of time allocated to staff development. (However although it was available in theory, it was not necessarily always accessible and hence was not used to its full). This gave 'space' for the partnership to flourish.
• The planning format outlined by the funder encouraged partners to plan ahead for the development of their capacities. This gave the partners the opportunity to see how their capacities were evolving.

Table 4.2: Selected Outputs from the Link

DATE	OUTPUT
1992–1998	Changes in attitude and behaviour of directly and indirectly involved CRDT and CDS staff regarding gender equity within their organisations and their training and consultancy practice
1992–1998	Skills acquired and enhanced by CDS and CRDT staff in workshop planning, materials production, delivery, documentation and evaluation of the workshops
1992–1998	Arabic documentation of workshop materials and resources used in them
1992–1998	The effectiveness of the two organisations has been increased by staff exposure to working in the Link partners' organisations
1992–1998	An expanded portfolio of work for both organisations
1995 and 1997	Training Manuals for Gender Awareness in Development and Organisational Effectiveness from a Gender Perspective
1996	Training modules for Gender and SMEs
1998	Two papers written on the History and Significance of the Link; Organisational Effectiveness from a Gender Perspective
1996 and 1997	Project proposals x 3 (2 x CDS/CRDT and 1 x CDS), including Logical Framework
1998	Outline Gender Checklists for Training and the Project Cycle

BUILDING THE CAPACITY OF OTHER ORGANISATIONS

Working on gender training activities in Egypt was very timely. The preparation leading up to the UN Conference on Population and Development, and its implementation in Cairo, brought to the fore the importance of integrating more fully women in development. The interest to know more about WID and GAD generated the demand for training on women, gender and development.

The training material developed by CDS and CRDT in collaboration with other partner organisations such as the Near East Foundation (NEF) was used by a number of other training organisations. In that respect one can say that the partnership contributed to building the knowledge of other organisations in gender training.

The demand for gender training stemmed from intermediary NGOs (support service rather than grass-roots organisations) and the donor agencies. This explains why the initial training delivered by CDS/CRDT mainly targeted this group. The topic was gender awareness and the discussion revolved around its relevance and meaningfulness in the context of the Arab world.

In contrast, community-based organisations which had limited donor exposure, did not expressly articulate the need to learn about and discuss gender issues, and independent of donor-funded activities, CDS and CRDT were out of their financial reach. Although the need was not expressed, it was felt that bringing the gender debate to the grass-roots level would help address the role of grass roots NGOs, their linkages with the community and the management of their activities. In this case, the training did not respond to a need but it certainly offered an opportunity to shed light on the potential of grass-roots organisations in community development. It helped the grass-roots organisations to reflect on the changes required in their current management practices and programme activities in order to play a more effective role in community development.

The partnership built the capacity of CDS/CRDT to reach outward to the wider community. The activities carried out were timely, useful and meaningful. They either fell within the trend of promoting knowledge about gender or they highlighted new opportunities for organisation effectiveness.

During training events, CRDT and CDS networked with grass-roots organisations and intermediary NGOs. But the partners did not take advantage of the possibility to translate these links into more formal and long-term networks. This may have hindered the progress of awareness about, and understanding of, the contribution of a gender perspective in community development.

MAIN ISSUES AFFECTING THE PARTNERSHIP

Sustainability

The sustainability of the partnership was affected by two main factors. These were both the purpose of the Link and how this impacted on the motivation of the people working within the partnership. The partnership formed around the subject of gender. This was new and interesting for CDS, and had relevance for work being currently carried out. For the staff development perspective of CRDT, coming to grips with gender training in practice in the Arab world was invaluable experience. With such a difficult subject to tackle, the possibilities for development and progress were not quickly exhausted. In fact there is not yet a feeling of 'well, we cracked it!' amongst the team partners and so the impetus to enquire still remains.

More than this, the subject-matter bred a need to look inwards at the heart of ourselves and our organisations and created in us a further necessity to address our approach to development and try to work this through from a gender perspective. Becoming involved in these questions, while trying to design, deliver and evaluate training would inevitably draw up large barriers between team workers and either force the partnership apart or draw the teams closer together. The personal time put into relationships between the partners further ensured that delicate questions could be addressed and thus further strengthened the teamwork. The challenge of the topic maintained a high involvement in the joint effort involved in achieving the outputs. This showed that partners were individually and internally motivated to continue the partnership.

Growth

The potential to grow close exists in the form of project concept notes which would require the partnership to standardise many administrative and financial systems as well as devote greater amounts of time to working together. However none has yet been accepted and many other factors seem presently to weaken the possibilities of the relationship growing.

Despite all the discussion and effort within the activity teams, there were certain aspects of the partnership which did not achieve their potential and may have thus limited the extent to which the partnership could grow in the future. Partners had the set-aside time and 'legitimacy' to be working within each other's organisations. But they failed to address and ascertain highly significant gender mainstreaming changes for our organisations. Although attempts were made to introduce 'action plans for change', neither partner has achieved this policy to date. Given legitimacy and funding, this would be a useful avenue for future exploration.

Another limitation on the growth of the partnership was the kind of external, financial support the partners were able to rely on. While the support was much appreciated, it was so limited as to ensure that the Link could never be a priority to those managing self-financing organisations. This meant that partners were always rushed and juggling several activities at one time. It was not only the amount that was limiting but the way in which it was budgeted – for travel or for training activities rather than for staff time.

Another donor support issue is that of monitoring and how this affected the partnership. The outputs expected were not always those achieved and the value of the actual outputs was not always understood. Those important outputs were mainly attitude-based and intangible. Future growth would depend on the ability to express these attitude-based indicators and to be able to legitimately evaluate the partnership on internal as well as external capacity-building indicators.

Ability to build capacity – both internally and externally

The partnership had two capacity-building elements to it. These were:

1. The internal development of capacity in each organisation, together with the partnership as a whole, and
2. The ability to provide meaningful capacity-building services to the communities which they serve.

Therefore there were two constituencies: the partners themselves and the community of NGOs and grass-roots organisations.

Servicing these dual constituencies was difficult to balance. There was an opportunity for working with others, which the partnership used. But taking up the offer meant delivering while still developing the partners' understanding from a somewhat experimental position. This could be seen by some as a weakness. However, the strength of this was in the openness partners had to change their perceptions as they undertook the training from a position of learning.

Overall the balance of capacity-building was in favour of the partners themselves. But this was related to the time available with which they had to work together. Given longer periods, such as the legitimacy of implementing a project, it is likely that the partners would work more with the external constituency.

CONCLUSIONS

This chapter has concentrated on the experiences of two not-for-profit organisations, which worked together over a number of years. While reflections have raised questions and pointed to the way in which these two partners could work together in the future, there are also some wider lessons to be learned about North/South partnerships.

Main Issues in North/South Partnerships

1. A partnership which is approach-based but practice-oriented may have the greatest potential to achieve a dual role of internal capacity-building and external servicing of the needs of the community.

2. There would seem to be limited value in sponsoring a partnership which has no external expression of its learning. The same applies the other way around, where only the external services are monitored. Reflection without the hope of learning, of transformation of self/partnership or organisation, can lead to a lack of congruency. And yet this is the experience of many partnerships. Greater congruency may be achieved by centring a partnership on a particular issue and examining its implications internally and in the surrounding community. However, there needs to be a balance between focusing on internal capacity-building and growth, and the ability to service the needs of the community. Experience of one feeds the other.

If North/South capacity-building partnerships are to be of value, then they need to internally reflect the processes and values that they are addressing in the community. In pursuing what we felt to be appropriate, we were not always as participatory in our enquiry as we needed to be; we set the agenda more than we could have done had we actively sought the opinions of, and worked with, the grass-roots organisations in our community. We have realised that we need to address immediate needs but also strategic issues related to how work is done, not only what should be done.

3. Links and partnerships that have been unsatisfactory both to the partners themselves and to their wider constituents, have often tried to have a dual role but have foundered on: a) the limited depth of the subject they explore together; b) the limited nature of their common interests as organisations and c) the unequal power relationship they share.

In these three aspects the CDS/CRDT partnership has been most fortunate. The organisations have:

- no funding relationship;
- mutual respect for each other and interdependence to provide a useful and meaningful service;
- common interests to develop staff, their portfolios, to survive in the marketplace and also to contribute to community development practice;
- strength, because they were drawn together over a subject which is so core and so complex as to cause a quick failure of the partnership once the surface of the subject had been scratched, or a deep bond because of the

personal and organisational values and attitudes which had to be addressed to progress the capacity-building.

4. Viable North/South partnerships do not just happen! They may need external support from a funder to enable them to justify the time and effort that is required for developing the personal relationships and the partnership agenda. For this the funders need to build sufficient time into their commitment and encourage them to look and plan forward

5. For North/South partnerships to flourish and have the capacity to be actors in strengthening civil society, funders need to note that the indicators by which the partnerships could be measured must include those intangible, attitude and process-based outputs and not just the activities. Without this, the struggling partnership may appear to have failed in the short term, where in reality much has been achieved on the way to changing attitudes, establishing new systems and developing new areas of work.

6. Funders should also note the basis on which they award funds. Alternative funding mechanisms have either focused on covering the travel costs of visits for joint planning and delivery, or the costs of delivering training programmes. For those, like CRDT and CDS, who need to cover their staff time, there are likely to be negative ramifications should there be insufficient funds over a long period. It is unlikely that both the entire organisations will be involved at any one time and those who work in the partnership will have no other responsibilities. If so, it will fall to other staff members to carry the work of the partners. This cannot happen indefinitely. It would be of help if funders could consider a grant to the organisation or consider funding staff time.

7. The overwhelming agreement within our partnership is that it has been worthwhile for us individually and as organisations. The partnership has offered those of us in the North and South new insights and opportunities.

The authors would like to acknowledge that without the hard work and support of the following women and men, this chapter would not have been written: Mary Surridge, Senior Lecturer, CRDT; Samaa Sayed and Fatma Mosallem, CDS; Hamdi Qenawi, IED Cairo; Dr Montasser Kamal, Canada; Ali Abd-el Aal, freelance consultant, Egypt; Mohmmed Abdel Hafiz, NEF Cairo; and David Pierce, DW&D Consulting, UK.

Chapter 5

'Stealing People's Decisions is Wrong!'

Raj Patel

> This chapter focuses on the relational element of capacity-building highlighting the importance of capacity-building being a two-way process. Raj Patel explores this concept by using a model of 'the mutual ladder' of capacity-building and by comparing two practical examples, one between a commercial financial services organisation and Indian NGOs and another between an international NGO and its networked partners in the South. He concludes that capacity-building MUST be mutual for the sake of all concerned.

INTRODUCTION

This chapter, when it was delivered as a paper at the conference, was entitled 'Reverse Capacity-Building'. Even if one does not agree with the sentiment of the new title I am certain that it is considered less dull. The title is a quote that has stuck in my mind since reading an article by Charles Handy. Handy explains that 'all managers are tempted to steal their subordinates' decisions'[9]. Then he pronounces the title judgement on such a crime. Coincidentally, I am reminded of an incident that occurred at about the same time as Handy wrote his paper. On my arrival to address a meeting on the topic of racial justice in Britain, I was warmly greeted by the co-ordinator who expressed her gratitude at my travelling so far. In a well-meaning comment, aimed at making me feel more comfortable amongst an entirely white audience, I was informed: 'Of course, we are not racist, we treat everyone as if they were white!' Stealing decisions can be innocent and its motive even to be supportive.

The development sector is a well-meaning sector that has learned that char-

[9] C. Handy, 1992, 'Balancing Corporate Power: A New Federalist Paper'.

itable acts must be replaced or at least accompanied by acts of empowerment
that lead to dignity and democratisation. My assertion is that we can move one
step further, realising and relating in a manner that acknowledges the necessity
of decisions to originate and be expedited both in the 'North' and the 'South'.
My emphasis for such a partnership is based on both grounds of common
humanity and professionalism (for proper impact and efficiency of projects and
programmes such mutuality is essential). To this end I offer the experiences, so
far, of two very different organisations, one from the commercial sector, Allied
Dunbar (Zurich Financial Services Group), and the other from the civil society
sector, Opportunity International (an international NGO). The common ground
for both is that they are in finance: OI in micro-finance and AD/ZFS in personal and organisational finance. In this chapter I also suggest a measurement tool,
a ladder, with which to gauge what level of mutuality has been achieved in
North-South partnerships and their projects.

EMERGING CONCEPTS AND RELATIONSHIPS

Without attempting to organise or list hierarchically the terms used in this arena
of mutuality the following are some common ones: reverse agenda, reverse participation, reverse capacity-building, reverse learning, reverse transformation,
reverse delegation, reverse powers and mirrored standards. The commercial
sector tends to use well-established words such as 'federalism' or more modern
words such as 'subsidiarity' whereby the relation is measured against where
power resides – in the case of subsidiarity it belongs at the lowest possible point
in the organisation.

The first of these common terms 'reverse agenda' was introduced by Riddell
and Bebbington in their paper exploring direct funding to Southern NGOs from
official agencies[10]. This report observes this non-intermediary type of relationship, commenting, 'in practice some donors ... have involved NGOs and grass-
roots organisations in the design, planning and monitoring of bilateral activities
... termed a process through which donors foster a *reverse agenda*'. They concur that the involvement of NGOs in the implementation countries from the
start does lead to a heightened impact of the interventions, 'a number of studies suggest that this type of interaction is perhaps the most effective way for
donors to consider interacting with NGOs'. This interaction with Southern
NGOs was in fact phrased as a clear recommendation that would allow for
exposure of the donor's personnel and therefore lead to appropriate policy and

[10] R. Riddell and A. Bebbington, 1995, 'Developing Country NGOs and Donor Governments:
Report to ODA'.

programmes – in fact, particularly, to influence the overall thrust of ODA's (now DFID) aid programme. The recommendation reads '... to ... expose ODA to the *reverse agenda* – opening up its aid programme further to the influence and input of NGOs and aid-recipient beneficiaries'. Such exposure additionally moves the culture of the organisation as its individuals influence policies as well as bring a new interpretation to the organisation's mission.

At the different level of intermediary relationship, that between the Southern NGO and community-based organisation, Alan Fowler extrapolates the concept and discusses 'reverse participation'[11]. Fowler emphasises its essentialness in the consolidation stage whereby not only is the likelihood of the success of the present project increased but it is also an investment deposited into future programmes. He also describes how such participation is vital in both delivery and evaluation: 'The principle of *reverse participation* ... Achieving shifts in relative power over decisions is the critical factor in the second stage [involving partnering, capacity-building and integration] of an intervention, complemented by mutually negotiated performance benchmarks'. In agreeing measurements of the success of projects, especially in recognising qualitative outcomes, the cobwebs in donors' minds are often, quite simply, blown away as there is acceptance of, if not submission to, how transformation is gauged at the most basic levels. The social accounting and auditing method has tried to mechanise and give authority to such approaches.

The view of INTRAC is a bold, yet sane, insistence that an indicator of genuine capacity-building of a Southern partner is the consequential and significant capacity-building of the Northern partner. If Northern NGOs are really serious about the organisational development of their partners they would seek to 'take the plank out of their own eye first'. Put another way, as in one of INTRAC's occasional papers: 'how can we teach others to fish, if we do not know how to fish ourselves?'[12] Although this quote illustrates a technical capacity it is applicable too in terms of other aspects of organisational activity. For example, three key areas of Southern NGO organisational capacity are governance, financial management and personnel development. It is not unknown and arguably increasingly likely from a South Asian perspective, that the Southern partners' financial management ability, at least of the medium-to-larger NGOs, may be superior to the Northern donor NGOs. In fact there is a significant proportion of Southern NGOs with operational budgets that are larger than their Northern counterparts. Similarly, I have on occasion calculated the average period of relevant experience of an organisation's staff and this has been significantly high-

---

[11] A. Fowler, 1997, 'Striking a Balance: A Guide to Enhancing the Effectivenesss of NGOs in International Development'.
[12] R. James, 1994, 'Strengthening the Capacity of Southern NGO Partners'.

er in the case of the Southern partners. Despite these qualifications, experience of North-South relations still demonstrates (though perhaps less so now) that when things go wrong blame is firmly placed at the door of the Southern NGO. For example when funds are delayed in reaching the Southern partner or they are not utilised efficiently by the Northern partner, excuses have the effect of scapegoating the distant partner. The antithesis here is therefore to build capacity, by example, in both directions – to establish a culture of learning, not blame.

The South and East Asia Consultation of the International Forum on Capacity-Building identified a list of benefits of SNGO-NNGO collaboration. This list is undergirded with the ease of which South-North and South-South communication can occur due to the major advances in information management and transfer. The IFCB/SEAC discusses 'enabling mutual learning from experiences' and gives examples of positive impact[13]:

1. Consensus on development priorities – better clarity of issues of development problems and priorities.
2. Networking in the North – with other development organisations that appreciate the global uniformity of issues.
3. Partnership in advocacy and lobbying on environmental and women's issues – towards a joint and effective approach on these and other issues of common concern.
4. Development of business – enabling and enhancing the social responsibility of the corporate sector by its investment in the development sector.
5. Development of government – increasing programmatic relationship between NGOs and government.

A common (mis) perception remains that 'Southern NGOs only want money!' A recent study on partnership viewed from Southern perspectives, with 233 organisational responses from the South and North, concludes that '.. the major concerns raised by the Southern development professionals points not to increased funding, but rather increased transparency and mutual respect ... both the North and South would be better placed to understand the constraints and complexities of each other's conditions. For the South, understanding the realities of their Northern partners and their relationship to donors .. might provide some insight into why their own relationship with donors is so complex.'[14] Although this conditional refutation against Southern NGOs being donor-led

[13] PRIA/IIRR, 1998, 'Politics of Capacity-Building'.
[14] S. Milne and D. Muchunguzi, 1995, 'Perspectives on the South: A Study of Partnership'.

stands, there are complexities at the SNGO level too and often their maturation in relationship must parallel the power and responsibility sharing encouraged by their Northern partners.

In a similar vein, 20 African NGOs more recently launched the Harare Declaration on Development Relationships. This declaration makes clear and separate suggestions for both Southern and Northern NGOs in order to fulfill its four points, declaring:

1. The time is ripe for Southern NGOs to take control of the development agenda in their own countries;
2. Change in development relationships is both necessary and inevitable;
3. Relationships should be based on mutual transparency and accountability;
4. There should be effective and meaningful dialogue between Southern and Northern NGOs.[15]

A useful reflection as we look at changing relationships and urge the above style of collaboration, is to consider the existing and potential effects of official (governmental bilateral or multilateral) funding that bypasses the intermediary Northern NGO (and indigenous government) and reaches the Southern NGO. This growing trend may provide concern particularly for NNGOs and the new type of role and relationship they enter into as a consequence. According to an INTRAC study of the impact of this shift:

> Perhaps the most disturbing effect of direct funding has been to transform the role of Northern NGOs from being partners working in solidarity with the South to being either partners in the sub-contracting chain or becoming themselves direct competitors against Southern NGOs for funds, and frequently the favoured partners of the aid agencies.[16]

The mutual approach provides a dignified and dignifying exegesis from the growing incidences of the inevitabilities of charitable organisations becoming cut-throat competitors. This is not solely between Northern and Southern actors but also within the Northern organisations. The struggle for resolution swings between proper space for and recognition of indigenous partners within an international network or building up a franchise structure with fund holders dic-

---

[15] Transform, 1998, 'The Harare Declaration: Challenging Relationships and Redressing the Power Imbalances Between Northern and Southern NGOs'.
[16] INTRAC, 1998, 'Direct Funding from a Southern Perspective: Strengthening Civil Society?'.

tating the development philosophy and activity. Some attempt is seen at doing this, not just by the international NGOs, but also, possibly more concerted, by official agencies. The Canadian International Development Agency's Policy Branch in 2000 launched its handbook for CIDA's project and programme officers, executive agencies and development partners. This, along with other work in conjunction with the World Bank's Indigenous Knowledge for Development Initiative will provide 'practical guidance on how indigenous knowledge can be better incorporated into project development and environmental assessment'[17]. This really is only a beginning and falls within the lower rungs of the 'Mutual Ladder' below. It seems quite evident that in order to avert the above-mentioned types of legalistic service level agreements and unhealthy competition a more radical approach to the mutuality is needed, hence the rungs of the ladder must be climbed proactively.

---

[17] P. Croal, 2000, 'Traditional Ecological Knowledge and its Integration into CIDA Programing'.

THE MUTUAL LADDER

Below is a tool for measuring the level of mutual capacity-building achieved between organisations (lowest level at bottom of ladder) in their working partnership. It is in the form of a ladder and therefore should be read from bottom-up to determine the rung your partnerships have reached.

Joint Ownership	*Equal and joint authority and responsibility for achieving mission within common philosophy*
Solidarity	*Advocating partner with external agencies, even at a cost or consequence*
Accountability	*Reporting and replying to all questions becomes a positive and compulsory interaction*
Management and design	*Voting board member exchange and active participation in programme development*
Evaluation	*Involvement in monitoring and evaluation – assessing the impact and effectiveness of tasks*
Transparency	*Openness concerning all matters of organisation e.g. board member exchange*
Advising	*A formal role allowing new perspective and experience e.g. organisational appraisals*
Training and Consultancy	*Development education and other matters such as MIS*
Assignments	*For technical aspects, research and personal development*
Exchanges	*Exposure visits between partners that include self-learning rather than appraisal*
Representation	*Making specific and regular inputs on a standing request and listed issues*
Consultation	*Being consulted about issues, but input may not be used fully*
Information Sharing	*Exchange of information, case studies and reports*

CASE STUDIES

Allied Dunbar/Zurich Financial Services

The AD/ZFS India Programme was initiated in 1994. The AD/ZFS Community Trust dates back to 1981 and is administered by their Community Affairs Department which, each year, commits approximately GB £ 2.5 million from profits and GB £ 1 million donated by its staff along with their time and skills. The first social accounting report of the India programme covered 1994–1996 and recommended that the Programme should 'develop and implement an approach to reverse learning'[18]. This finding has given the India Programme opportunities to better develop the concept of partnership. Discussion with the various stakeholders identified some suggestions for reverse learning which are encapsulated in the chart below. This chart was drawn up using the above mutual ladder to describe the stages in reverse learning. The second social accounting report[19] covering the two years 1997–1999 confirms progress made as well as further opportunities in developing reverse learning.

---

[18] Allied Dunbar, 1997, 'The India Programme Social Accounting Report (1994-1996).
[19] Zurich Financial Services Community Trust Ltd., 2000, 'The India Programme Social Accounting Report (1997-1999).

'Reverse Learning' Stages	Definition within the India Programme	Achieved to date for development of learning across all partners	Possible opportunities
Equal partnership	• Joint responsibility for achievement of goals	• Individual partnerships documented by MOUs • Partners network	• Use the current partners more directly in the identification of new partners/programme development • Advisory Group **Constraint:** Ultimate responsibility for budget and therefore right of veto for the Programme lies with BAFSCT
Accountability and Transparency	• Shared accountability and openness	• Partners network Use of social accounting techniques	• Develop totally transparent communication • Partner social accounting
Evaluation and improvement	• Involvement in monitoring and evaluation	• Social accounting for India Programme	• Involvement of the partners network to identify solutions to social accounting recommendations
Part of Sub-committees or interest groups / advisory roles / consultation	• Active participation in the development of activities	• Partners network has input to India Programme through consultation	• Use partner representatives as members of the India Programme Advisory Group

Training	• Sharing and transfer of skills and experience	• Allied Dunbar assignees working with partners in India • Partners staff attending training courses when in the UK • Visits hosted in Swindon for partners visiting the UK • Partners sharing training opportunities e.g. consultancy skills etc.	• Partners working with assignees to develop training workshops to commit to offering them to other partners if appropriate • Regularly circulate list of assignments so that partners can share experience as appropriate • Publish Allied Dunbar training programme and encourage partners staff to attend courses if in the UK
Exchanges, assignments	• Personal development for staff through assignment	• Partners funded to attend appropriate training courses in the UK • Allied Dunbar staff assignments with partners	• Development of concept for partner staff development through assignment • Assignments between partners **Constraint** Budget not currently available for this through the India Programme (partners meeting to identify how this might be resourced)
Development education	• Learning through experiencing new cultures	• Induction meetings for assignees • Informal partner networks	• More *ad hoc* sharing of information/ experience
Information Exchange	• Sharing of information	• Partners meeting, sharing of approaches and experiences	

Allied Dunbar / Zurich Financial Services opted for a comprehensive and continued approach to reverse learning. The benefits are spelled out in the social accounting report and the programme continues to expand with additions observed such as determined South-South partnerships amongst the AD/ZFS partners.

Opportunity International

The Opportunity International Network has origins dating back to 1971. It has worked in 29 Southern countries with one or more partners and there are seven Northern countries with a 'support' partner. Its focus is micro-enterprise development, and in 1998 162,712 jobs resulted from 124,462 loans (approx. US$ 32.4 million loaned).

In October 1997, after two years' work of the Network Design Council, a Network Board, the ultimate decision-making body of the network, was formed of twelve members with six from the 'North' and six from the 'South' (incidentally the first Chair was African). The Network Board at its first meeting in February 1988 developed a 5-Year Vision Statement outlining outreach, quality and impact. The impact is summarised as '... empowering poor clients in such a manner that they become agents of transformation in their own communities'.

In June 1998, a session on transformation was organised as part of a board meeting, at which senior staff members were also present, to discuss transformation. A support partner input outlined the 'Suzy Tree' – illustrating transformation as opening out like the branches of a tree, with each branch representing one of the following: individual transformation, household transformation, business transformation and community transformation. The roots of the tree tapping into the donor sap facilitating the weekly interaction loan officer and client (the trunk). The implementing partner representatives, from Africa and Asia, were asked to provide case studies for such transformation, which they did. Furthermore a challenge was set to view the Suzy Tree as an upside-down illustration and the US participants (approximately 20) were asked to think of case studies of 'reverse-transformation'. After small group work, 18 case studies were presented at the plenary and the proportions in the following categories were indicated mainly as 'first-branch' experience:

Personal/Family transformation	11	(61%)
Work/Organisational transformation	5	(28%)
Community/society transformation	2	(11%)

In 1999 the OI Network organised a workshop of its international staff, those employed by the Network but working in 'implementing countries'. In a concluding session it was agreed that there should be concerted effort at policy level and programme level to 'break the glass wall' that exists. The author, the Managing Director of the OI Network stated: 'If we are to ... fulfil our mission, we must recognize that a *glass wall* exists within our Network'. The *glass wall* hinders knowledge and expertise from passing back and forth between Support Partners and Regional Offices on one side and Implementing Partners on the other. Implementing Partners develop knowledge about their own local contexts and how their programs apply to it.[20]

This was then followed up with a consultation paper and a well-participated e-mail conference for all partners in the Network. The Network Board met having received an analysis of responses and reached a directive that seeks to move towards breaking the glass wall by better equalising the decision-making and particularly moving the technical support services nearer to the project implementation. This is phrased as 'career ladders rising toward Implementing Partners'. It was agreed too that the accreditation of implementing partners should be done concurrently with the accreditation of support and regional partners. The latter, however, has met with some level of difficulty, if not resistance. Exchange of board members (North-South and South-North) has also been agreed and received positively by some implementing partner boards by making them voting members rather than observers/advisors. A restructuring is in process in order to source the technical inputs in Southern countries. These are clear intentions that lead the participants onto the higher rungs on the mutual ladder. In many ways the act of putting these intentions into practice is a harder challenge than making the policy decisions.

MIRRORED STANDARDS

The case studies of Allied Dunbar/ZFS and Opportunity International Network provide interesting approaches to mutual capacity-building. The AD/ZFS approach is from programme to policy while the OI Network approach is from policy to programme. Their approaches ironically seem reversed when the nature of the two organisations are qualified – one corporate and the other NGO.

The early impressions indicate that a lasting capacity-building intervention requires a change of culture in the organisations and networks. Whether it is best achieved by a single approach or both approaches together remains to be seen. However, as stated clearly by a Southern executive director, *'it's about time that the support partners themselves mirrored and adhered to the standards they expect of us'*.

For SNGOs, NNGOs, official agencies, corporate donors and individual donors to achieve such a change of culture will require a step of 'unfreezing' the old cul-

---

[20] L. Reed, 1999, 'Breaking the Glass Wall' Opportunity International Network.

ture before taking on the new. The trend is that the Southern partners as they scale-up and develop their capacities, are larger and more complex than their Northern partners who so far have insisted on delivering the capacity-building interventions. This, often with little or no experience in actually developing or overseeing an organisation, is a clear example of an area that needs to be 'unfrozen'.

A useful tool for the transfer of mutual capacity-building is an intermediary such as a Southern NGO support organisation with suitable link person/s. A recent tangible example is around the lengthy stalemate of the legal status of micro-finance institutions. The support partners have globally acknowledged this as a problem for 'ages' but have not been able to move positively with it. A Southern NGO support organisation jointly with the regional partner has provided a far-reaching study with detailed recommendations of how this may be addressed in the Southern country concerned as well as provide a parallel for recommendations for support countries – 'A Will Needing a Way'[21.]

A further example is how the India Programme of AD/ZFS's mutual capacity-building concept/practice and social auditing aspects have been incorporated into AD/ZFS's wider community affairs programmes. Additionally these are now being introduced to the other members of their group (which includes Zurich Financial Group of Companies, Eagle Star and Threadneedle).

CONCLUSION – WHO NEEDS WHOM MORE?

The question of who benefits from partnerships in development can be clearly answered – *we all do and, and when we all do, the impact is magnified.*

The Southern NGO partners often are slower at approaching a mutuality in the relationship, even when the Northern partners not only see the benefits but have the will to promote such a partnership. A significant de-freezing of age-old inferiority or dependence organisational mentality needs to be addressed and can only be initiated by the Southern NGO itself.

The assumption of equality in relationships is proved as a necessity. However, a question continues to be asked: 'Who needs whom more?' Can efficient Southern NGOs shop around for the types of donor/NNGO they can work with jointly? Can Northern NGOs find the SNGOs that concur with their philosophy and mission and still deliver the volume and quality of projects that will meet the disbursement targets?

The development and commercial wisdom echo a loud sound of mutual capacity-building equally for the sake of all concerned.

---

[21] AIAMED/OI India, 1998, 'A Will Needing a Way: Legal and Procedural Constraints in Micro-Finance'.

Part Four

Capacity-Building at Societal Level

Chapter 6

Building Capacity of Alliances in Mozambique: Developing the 'Agenda for Action for Children'

Roy Trivedy
Save the Children (UK)

This chapter focuses on capacity-building interventions at a societal level, rather than just within or between two organisations, and on the role of international organisations in promoting the development of 'An Agenda for Action for Children'. It is based on the experience of the Save the Children Alliance and UNICEF in Mozambique in 1998. Furthermore, it seeks to contribute to the debate on the changing role of NGOs in a global future by sharing a new and innovative experience of collaboration between government, civil society, NGOs and international organisations.

The aim of the chapter is to share key lessons learned from the process of mobilising child-serving organisations to more effectively support the development of children and youth as an integral part of the country's development process. The chapter is divided into three sections. Section 1 explains the reasons for the development of 'the Agenda' and the intended outcomes of this process. Section 2 outlines key elements of the Agenda for Action and the processes that are being used to mobilise society. Section 3 examines some of the lessons learned from this experience and also examines the role of international and national organisations in supporting this process.

This is an example of an alliance of a number of different organisations attempting to build capacity at a societal level.

The author is grateful to Mark Stirling, Anita Menete, Joao Jussar and many others who have provided valuable advice and comments on this paper. Any errors that remain are, of course, my sole responsibility.

INTRODUCTION

As in other countries, the work of NGOs in Mozambique has come under greater scrutiny over the past few years. In part this has been an outcome of the changing global context confronting NGOs as well as changes within Mozambique. The shift within Mozambique, from emergency work to 'long-term development' has meant that while a large number of new national NGOs have been registered in the past two or three years, the activities of NGOs have also come under greater criticism from the various quarters. Partly as a result of this, in 1998 the government introduced a new law to regulate and more close-ly monitor the work of international NGOs. New legislation to regulate the activities of national NGOs is also likely to be introduced in the future. These changes have been accompanied by a greater reluctance on the part of key donors, including DFID, to fund directly NGO projects, preferring instead to fund government programmes.

In this context, a key challenge confronting NGOs (both national and inter-national) has been to re-assess their strategies and traditional ways of operating and to find more effective ways of forging partnerships and alliances to achieve their objectives. One example of this is a new and innovative experience of col-laboration between government, civil society, NGOs and international organi-sations in Mozambique.

THE DEVELOPMENT OF THE AGENDA FOR ACTION

In February 1998 the three Save the Children Alliance organisations in Mozambique (UK, Norway and the USA) and UNICEF organised a two-day retreat for senior staff. The aim of the retreat was to share the existing work and strategies of each of our organisations and to identify possible areas of closer co-operation and collaboration to more effectively build commitment and capacity within Mozambican society to ensure the fulfilment of children's rights. The group agreed that as part of the above process, priority attention would need to be devoted to the development of an Agenda for Action for Mozambican Children (founded on a broadly based understanding of the situation of children and a consensus on the 'rights gaps' and priorities for action). Several collabo-rative actions were agreed to further this process. These included:

- the provision of financial and technical support for the preparation of the Government of Mozambique's Report to the UN Committee on the Rights of the Child;

- the development and implementation of a national strategy for child rights training; and
- the development of an advocacy and communications strategy to support the 'Agenda for Action'.

Following the initial agreement, in July 1998, the Save the Children Alliance, UNICEF and the Fundacao Para O Desenvolvimento da Communidade (FDC) organised a workshop in Maputo on 'The Development of a Child Rights Culture' in Mozambique. This workshop was timed to coincide with the start of the preparation of the government of Mozambique's Report to the Committee on the Rights of the Child[22]. More than thirty organisations participated in the workshop.

One major conclusion from this workshop was that participants highlighted the human costs of not fulfilling children's rights in Mozambique. A strong consensus was reached that effective action to respond to this situation could only emerge from a combined, well oriented and motivated effort of child-serving organisations and Mozambican society as a whole. A large number of child-serving organisations in Mozambique – within civil society, the NGO community, international organisations and government – therefore expressed the need to strengthen co-ordination and collaboration and to improve the focus of their efforts to have a more substantive effect in fulfilling the rights of children.

To orient and provide a framework for this collaboration, the idea of developing an 'Agenda for Action for Mozambican Children' was agreed as a priority. Staff from the Save the Children Alliance and UNICEF agreed to develop a draft concept paper on the scope and purpose of the Agenda. This paper formed the basis for more detailed discussions with Dr Graca Machel of FDC, other key individuals and organisations. Through this process, greater understanding and commitment to the development and implementation of an Agenda for Action was built.

---

[22] The Save the Children Alliance and UNICEF are involved in providing technical support and funding for the government of Mozambique in preparing its report for the Child Rights Committee. This workshop grew out of the process of CRC Reporting and the Alliance, and UNICEF's concern that the process of preparing the report needed to be inclusive and participatory (involving NGOs and civil society as well as government) and that it needed to reflect accurately the situation of children in the country.

Why do we need an Agenda for Action?

Many reasons were advanced as to why an Agenda such as this was needed. They included:

- Children form a key group in Mozambican society. Approximately 55% of the population of Mozambique are under the age of 18. Many children and young people are especially vulnerable due to their age, maturity, gender, disability, poverty and other factors. Children's rights are frequently violated. Investing in the development of children now is not only a moral imperative but an investment for the future as it is likely to result in youth and adults that can take greater responsibility for their own development and that of Mozambique. The Agenda for Action will provide a framework for galvanising action to support the development of all children in Mozambique.

- Children are often forgotten or overlooked. With the rapid pace of development and change taking place in Mozambique the needs and rights of children have often been overlooked or forgotten in development planning and decision-making. By clarifying the priorities for action for children, the Agenda for Action will provide guidance on how to put children first in terms of decision-making in development and resource allocation.

- Children's own views are rarely sought. Children are rarely consulted about the development and implementation of policies and programmes that directly affect their lives. The Agenda will provide an opportunity to give children a voice in the development of plans and actions that influence their lives.

- Policies targeted at children are generally reasonable but their implementation is weak. Since peace (1992), government (at national and provincial levels) has been very active in developing policies and strategies to guide Mozambique's development and that of its people. While much has been achieved in establishing this enabling environment, more still needs to be done in implementing these policies, in ensuing that they bring direct, relevant and sustainable benefits to children, and in identifying critical gaps where policy and action is required. The Agenda could therefore be used as a tool for helping to operationalize national, provincial and organisational development plans and ensuring that these really do benefit children and their families.

- Capacities of child-serving organisations are spread thin and fragmented. With the wide range of development challenges and limited capacities of government and civil society to address these, there has been a tendency to spread and fragment organisational capacities, often resulting in frustration and the under-achievement of planned results. Child-serving organisations in Mozambique are also keen to build their capacities to work with and for children. The Agenda for Action would seek to focus attention on a limited number of priority areas for action.

- Cross-sectoral and govt/NGO/CSO/international agency co-ordination is weak. The lack of recognised agreement on priorities for action has frustrated efforts to strengthen linkages between government ministries, and between government, NGO, CSO and international partners. The Agenda for Action could provide a framework for facilitating this cross-sectoral and cross-organisational co-ordination and collaboration

Source: Extract from the Draft Concept Paper on the Agenda for Action – Prepared by the Save the Children Alliance and Unicef

The process of discussion and debate about the initial concept paper culminated in a second workshop in November 1998. Preparations for the workshop were co-ordinated by UNICEF, Alliance and FDC staff, with support from a UNICEF-sponsored consultant.

Approximately one hundred participants representing government, leaders within civil society, NGOs, international organisations and others participated in the workshop and made a commitment to work for the development and implementation of the Agenda. For most participants, this workshop represented a first attempt to forge a broad alliance of 'child-serving organisations' and to begin the process of creating a movement for the fulfilment of child rights in the country.

In the November workshop there was much discussion about whether the idea of creating a 'movement' was 'too ambitious'. Few participants had experience of developing a 'movement' in society such as the 'Agenda for Action'. For many government and NGO participants it represented a 'new' and unfamiliar approach in the Mozambican context. For others however, such as the Continuadores and the Organisation of Mozambican Women (OMM) the attraction of the Agenda lies in the kinds of partnership that are envisaged, the fact that this initiative will strengthen their other activities, the kinds of tools that this work will require and the focus on children and young people.

Outside of the formal discussions, some government officials and NGO representatives raised doubts about the dependability of the other 'partners in this new alliance' but agreed to 'wait and see'. There was also considerable discussion about the scope ('too broad and ambitious') and timing of this initiative. Additionally, with general elections due in Mozambique in 1999 some participants questioned whether it made sense to launch such an initiative in Mozambique at that time.

An important part of the November workshop involved the participation of twenty-four young people (from various organisations) on the second day. For many of the adult participants this was the first time that they had been involved in a meeting in which young people were also participants. The young participants played an active role in the discussions and also made recommendations for follow-up work (including ways of effectively involving young people in developing and implementing the Agenda).

After much discussion all participants eventually agreed that the situation in terms of the basic rights of children and young people in the country demanded an initiative such as the Agenda. The importance of 'child-serving organisations co-ordinating their activities and working for a common purpose was critically needed'. Moreover, the long-term nature of the plan and the objectives outlined in the Agenda concept paper were felt to be 'worth striving for' and 'achievable' (though it was agreed that the original timetable proposed in the concept paper would need to be revised).

It was agreed that the Agenda for Action would be a plan of action to guide and co-ordinate the efforts of all child-serving organisations to expand and accelerate work for the fulfilment of child rights in Mozambique. Furthermore, the Agenda for Action was to be a compact between government, civil society, non-governmental organisations and international organisations. It was also agreed that the Agenda would be used to guide advocacy, social mobilisation and programming efforts of organisations, groups, and individuals to achieve a defined set of objectives for children in Mozambique over the period 2000-2020. This period of time coincides with the government of Mozambique's existing plans for meeting key development objectives in the country. Participants agreed that as a compact, the priorities and strategies of the Agenda for Action would need to be reflected in national planning instruments (including the Five-Year Plan, General Budget and the Triennial Investment Plan), and the policies and practices of civil society (including parents, carers of children, youth and children), non-governmental organisations, and international development partners concerned about children's rights and welfare in Mozambique.

It was emphasised that since the Agenda for Action seeks to mobilise the support and commitment of a broad alliance of child-serving organisations, the process of its preparation must be <u>participatory and inclusive</u>. Moreover since much of the action to fulfil the needs and rights of children will be required at family and community levels and at organisational level, it will be imperative to promote public awareness and interest to act in the best interests of the child.

Since the Agenda for Action would be used to guide advocacy, mobilisation, programming and co-ordination efforts it was felt that it must be easily accessible, reader-friendly and relatively short. Participants agreed that it should be a document referred to by the president and senior government leaders, religious groups, NGOs and community-based organisations, co-operating agencies, government administrators and functionaries. As one participant expressed it...'*It must be a document that people remember, find useful and refer to.*'

Participants also agreed that since the purpose of the Agenda would be to guide efforts to fulfil children's rights, its structure should reflect the structure of the Convention on the Rights of the Child (with its four key sets of rights-survival, development, protection and participation). Moreover it was emphasised that the Agenda should focus on key actions to be undertaken at all levels in society over the period 2000–2020.

KEY ELEMENTS OF THE AGENDA

Seven priority elements have been agreed for preparation as part of the Agenda for Action. These are:

1. *Highlights of the situation of children* including a summary of the situation of children in Mozambique; a review of the policy environment and extent to which current policies and actions are responding to children's needs and rights; analysis of major 'rights gaps' to survival, development, protection and participation; and presentation of priorities for action for the period 2000–2010.

2. *The vision for and of Mozambican children* including a statement of what should be possible to attain for all Mozambican children (initially by 2010 and then beyond) and an outline of how Mozambican children and young people can be involved in shaping this vision for the future.

3. *Clear goals and strategies* including for each priority area for action clear goals and quantifiable/measurable time-bound targets which can be agreed to guide the planning and monitoring of progress.

4. *A framework for co-operation* which covers a definition by major goal and target, key strategies to be pursued and activities to be undertaken by key organisations, groups and interested individuals. This will also define how national planning instruments (such as the Five-Year Plan, Annual Budget and Sector Plans) will be used to explicitly put children first.

5. *A resource framework* which defines, by goal or target area, the resources required to attain agreed goals and targets from government and other sources.

6. *Methods for monitoring and progress assessment:* which defines how implementation of the Agenda will be monitored, and progress and lessons learned will be fed back into planning processes.

7. *Clear institutional arrangements* which define the organisations that agree to be involved, standards and principles of involvement, and how the implementation of the Agenda will be co-ordinated (through a 'Preparatory Commission').

In preparing the strategy to develop the Agenda for Action four key components have been identified. These are:

1. the need to develop an analysis of the existing situation of children in Mozambique, and an assessment children's rights (including the views of children and young people about their lives);

2. the importance of developing an information and communication strategy to promote awareness and understanding of child rights and society's obligation to fulfil children's rights;.

3. the importance of promoting discussion (amongst adults and children) to develop a vision of what 'should be attainable' for (all) Mozambican children by 2010 and, on the basis of this, identify priority goals and actions to achieve this condition; and

4. the need to facilitate a participatory process whereby the above learning, discussion and planning can be harnessed and captured in a statement of intent, and in concrete action plans reflected in the Agenda for Action. Progress in implementation of the action plan can then be monitored on a regular basis.

A provisional ten-step process for developing the Agenda for Action was agreed at the November workshop as follows.

Step 1   Conceptual development and coalition building involving key government officials, community leaders, organisations working with and for children, and others. After clarifying the concept and having the commitment of key leaders in society the group will approach the Prime Minister to seek approval and commitment on behalf of the Council of Ministers to launch the Agenda planning process as a vehicle to define the priorities and partnerships required for effective action to put children first.

Step 2   Establish leadership and co-ordination mechanisms through the formation of: (1) a Preparatory Commission, comprising representatives of government and the major child-serving organisations in Mozambique, to guide and co-ordinate the inputs of various involved organisations and to approve the final product; and (2) a Technical Task Force, located within the Ministry of Social Action to support and facilitate the Agenda preparation process.

101

Step 3   Undertake a situation and current response analysis about children in Mozambique .

Step 4   Design and implement a public information and communication strategy as part of a mobilisation process.

Step 5   Undertake sub-national (including four regional and district level) consultations to review the situation of children and the CRC report, and to discuss and agree on vision, goals and strategy and institutional arrangements to be included within the Agenda for Action.

Step 6   Prepare a first draft of Agenda for Action based on regional consultations.

Step 7   Hold a national workshop to present, discuss and further develop draft Agenda for Action.

Step 8   Prepare final copy of Agenda and submit to the Preparatory Commission for consideration.

Step 9   Once agreed at the Preparatory Commission, the Agenda will then be submitted for consideration and approval by the Council of Ministers.

Step 10   Launch of the AGENDA, as a *'social pact'* by the President and key leaders in society.

With careful planning and the support of a full-time Technical Working Group, it was envisaged that this process would be completed within a period of 12 months. Participants decided that all interested and committed child-serving organisations throughout the country should be invited to partake in the development of the Agenda for Action. It was recognised that the basis for the success of the Agenda would depend on the active participation of key organisations and individuals. It is therefore envisaged that government ministries, parliamentarians and political leaders, state institutions, leaders of civil society and religious organisations, non-governmental organisations, trade unions, the private sector, adults and children themselves would all form a part of this 'movement'.

The November workshop resolved that major vehicles for participation would be through the national and sub-national workshops to discuss child rights, the situation of children and priorities for action. These workshops would also involve children and young people at provincial and district levels.

In addition, it is intended that through the information and communication strategy on child rights, government, non-governmental organisations and community-based organisations would play an active part in building consciousness about citizens rights and obligations, and promoting public involvement in and support for the Agenda.

Participants at the November workshop agreed that the process of developing the Agenda for Action would be guided and overseen by a Preparatory Commission comprising a range of senior leaders in society and the leaders of 'child-serving organisations'. It was also agreed that the Preparatory Commission, and the work plan it endorses, would be implemented by a smaller Technical Working Group that will be situated in the Ministry of Social Welfare – but supported with additional technical capacity and resources.

Following the November workshop a number of concrete pieces of work to advance the Agenda had begun and by the beginning of April 1999 some significant steps had been taken towards the first four steps outlined above.

OUTCOMES AND LESSONS LEARNED

It is possible to conclude from the above that what has been achieved so far amounts to little more than a series of workshops, discussions, ideas and concepts! It is too early to say to what extent this process will result in genuine improvements in the lives of children and young people or what the long-range outcome will be in terms of the fulfilment of children's rights. Down the road we will have a clearer idea of the difficulties and constraints, as well as successes of this approach. The initial phase of this work has, however, resulted in some positive signs and raised critical challenges for the future. Some positive signs include the following:

• The willingness of government, NGOs and leaders in society to participated actively in and contribute to the development of the Agenda has been staggering. Within two months more than one hundred organisations and individuals (including government, key institutions, religious leaders, NGOs and young people) had committed themselves to work for its development and implementation.

• There is a growing 'ownership of the process' by various Mozambican organisations and individuals. There has also been a considerable amount of interest in this process on the part of some multilateral and bilateral aid agencies (including the World Bank and NORAD). Many individuals and organisations commented at the workshop in November that since July 1998 (when the first workshop was organised), there has been noticeably more collaboration between 'child-serving organisations'. Moreover, within many organisations (including Save the Children and UNICEF), the Agenda for Action has resulted in increased motivation and commitment amongst staff, and has created a sense of contributing to an active 'movement' in society. The Agenda for Action will provide a framework for collective and individual action and a basis for the development of a longer-term partnership between government and civil society for improving the lives of a majority of Mozambique's population (since children comprise more than 50% of the population). The challenge now is to continue the momentum that has been established and to build on this.

• The development and implementation of the Agenda for Action will involve the development of 'tools' to assist the process. A number of working groups with commitments from different organisations have been established including a group responsible for developing an advocacy strategy and appropriate tools to promote the Agenda. There is already considerable progress on the development of some of the tools. This includes the development of a Portuguese version of a Training Pack for Journalists on Interviewing Children (dissemination of this and the development of a national training strategy is now under way). Printing and dissemination of the Ministry of Social Welfare's policies related to children and of the Child Rights Convention has also commenced. A training manual in Portuguese on child rights, field tested in Mozambique, has also been developed and medium-term strategy for training key groups in society has also been developed and is now being implemented. A number of individuals have commented that the development of these tools has also increased capacity within their organisations to plan and implement such work.

Several organisations have indicated their wish to be involved in the work on the situation analysis of children. This entails using a variety of methods to highlight the diversity of children's lives in the country and the different childhoods that exist, children and young peoples aspirations for the future, as well as examining the implications of government policies relating to children. Some of this work has already begun and was developed further during 1999 (for example work on the implications of government expenditure on children[23]). The government's report for the UN Child Rights Committee was also scheduled to be completed by June 1999

---

[23] See for example S. Robinson and L. Biersteker (eds.), 1997, 'First Call: The South African Children's Budget'. There are plans to introduce similar methods as part of the work on the situation analysis of children in Mozambique in 1999.

and will contain much useful information about the situation of children. All of this promises to add innovative and exciting new methods of working effectively with and for children in Mozambique over the next few years.

- Another key change is the way in which children and young people are beginning to be viewed as development actors in their own right in Mozambique rather than just passive recipients of 'aid'. In the July 1998 workshop, children's participation in development was strongly emphasised by the Save the Children Alliance and UNICEF. With young people actively participating in the November workshop this was again reinforced. It has been noticeable that organisations that for many years have been working with children essentially as beneficiaries of projects have recently begun to consult and involve children and young people more effectively and to think more critically about their activities. An example of this is the work of the Rede de Criancas (Network of Children's Organisations) that focuses on work with street children in Maputo. The Rede has been involved in developing the Agenda for Action and in 1999 had begun to form a 'Children's Forum' with the idea of involving and informing children more effectively in its work.

    The increasing focus on children and young people in development has also brought to the fore the work of organisations such as Aro Juvenil (which works with young people on their priority issues including HIV AIDS). The increasing focus on children in development has also begun to influence work that in the past rarely involved consideration of children. For example, a number of research initiatives have begun in 1998 looking at issues of child poverty. The implications of macro-economic policies (including debt) on children is another area that is now being more carefully considered as part of the Poverty Alleviation Unit's work in the Ministry of Planning and Finance. UNICEF and Save the Children have also taken an initiative to ensure that the National Assembly considers the implications for children of the 'new constitutional arrangements that will come into force in 1999 (the process of revision of the Constitution is currently in progress'). More is needed to reinforce the message that children and young people must be treated as active participants in development rather than just passive recipients, but there is a good base to build on. It is no longer the case that only a few organisations are emphasising the importance of children's active participation in development.

- A key question that emerges from our reflections over the past year is the extent to which the work on the Agenda for Action has built capacity in Mozambican society for the fulfilment of child rights. There is evidence to suggest that the work on the Agenda has contributed to capacity-building within the Ministry of Social Action (responsible for co-ordinating the preparation of the government's report for the Child Rights Commission and a lead ministry for the development of the Agenda for Action). There is also some evidence to suggest that the work on the Agenda for Action has strengthened the capacity of some NGOs (this was specifically mentioned by organisations such as the Associacao Dos Amigos Da Crianca that took part in preparing the November workshop).

Perhaps more significant than its contribution to capacity-building, however, is the implication that the work on the Agenda for Action has (and potentially will have) for strengthening 'social capital' in Mozambique. By strengthening the relations between individuals, communities, organisations and government it has incredible potential to contribute to the individual and social well-being of a large section of the country's population. This could potentially be the major contribution of the Agenda that leads to improving the lives of children in Mozambique in the next twenty years.

- A key element of the 'success' so far of the process of developing the Agenda for Action has been that each of the organisations and individuals who have contributed to its development, have taken care to respect and value the contributions of others. This has not meant that there have been no disagreements between the various organisations and individuals about the best ways to advance the process. So far, however, it has proved possible to manage and resolve these differences (partly because of mutual respect and a strong sense of accountability to each other). This has been reinforced by the insistence that the process must remain inclusive and participatory. The Save Children Alliance, UNICEF and FDC have taken care to catalyse and provide leadership for the process but at the same time to ensure that the Agenda is not seen by others as being 'owned solely by these organisations'.

The challenge for development organisations (characterised by the work on the Agenda for Action) is to find ways of working together more effectively (whether as groups of diverse organisations – national and international or as individuals – adults, children, women, men, girls and boys) to promote and attain common goals.

Just as national and international NGOs are beginning to find new ways of working together more effectively in the process of developing the Agenda for Action, so too are UNICEF and the Save the Children Alliance. One participant at the November Workshop remarked, '*it is great to see your organisations working more closely together which was never the case in the past. It is pro-*

viding us [national NGOs] with more technical support and information'.
Collaboration between the Alliance and UNICEF has strengthened considerably at a global level over the past two years (though there is clearly more
room for further improvement). In Mozambique this has been especially evident
as the Alliance and UNICEF have sought to benefit and learn from each other's
work. Practical examples of this include work on 'Rights-based Programming',
Child Rights Training, work on HIV AIDS and child protection. For the
Alliance and UNICEF, this has led to more critical thinking within our organisations about our respective roles and activities. There is evidence to suggest
that this has helped to contribute more effectively to the achievement of our
mission statements. In the future the challenge will be to find ways of building
on the work that has started and to ensure that our partnership is further developed and strengthened.

SOME CONCLUDING THOUGHTS

In addition to the positive signs of progress mentioned above, there is however
also recognition of the critical areas that will need to be addressed in the next
period. These include:

• the need to develop mechanisms that can be used to ensure that children and
  young people (girls and boys) are genuinely involved in this process;

• the need for more work on ways of mobilising organisations and individuals
  in civil society (adults and children) to continue to support and develop this
  process;

• the need for much more work to mobilise state institutions and key office
  bearers to support this process;

• the need to ensure that the 'alliance for the Agenda' continues to strengthen
  and grow and that the mechanisms for leadership and co-ordination are
  established;

• the need to find ways of involving the media and the private sector in
  developing and promoting the Agenda;

• the necessity of finding ways of ensuring that the Agenda for Action
  becomes a national priority and not just confined to the work of specific
  organisations working in certain parts of the country; and

• the need to ensure that the impact of the Agenda on children's lives in Mozambique is properly monitored;

There are lots of expectations for the future. There is also an incredible impetus to develop and contribute to a process that will result in real improvements to the lives of the bulk of the population of the country for current and future generations.

Chapter 7

Learning from the NGOs in Central Asia

Anne Garbutt
INTRAC

This capacity-building programme is the most comprehensive example presented. While the other cases outline interventions focused on one level, and maybe permeating to another, the INTRAC capacity-building programme in Central Asia seeks to intervene simultaneously at all level – individual, organisational, inter-organisational and societal. It provides a useful comparison with other more focused programmes and introduces a very different context from the largely Africa-based cases presented so far. It takes place in the rarefied context of an emerging NGO sector from the ashes of former Soviet control.

INTRODUCTION

The purpose of the INTRAC [24] Institutional Development Programme of NGOs in Central Asia is to contribute to the process of democratic transition in Central Asia by supporting the emergence of a vibrant, effective and independent NGO sector in the region. INTRAC's involvement in Central Asia began in 1994 with an invitation from UNV/UNDP to design a community-based poverty alleviation programme for Kyrgyzstan.

This process led to the realisation that there was an absence of viable structures to work through and that the assumption by the multilateral agencies that with the collapse of the old state structures, local NGOs would take on the role of creating a new safety net for the vulnerable was going to be impossible with-

[24] INTRAC's programme of Institutional Development of NGOs in Central Asia, funded by The Know How Fund, Hivos and Novib started in April 1997 with the appointment of Anne Garbutt as the Programme Manager based in Oxford and Theresa Mellon, Project Manager based in Bishkek, Kyrgyzstan

out considerable input to the fledgling NGO sector.

Between 1994 and 1997, INTRAC worked with NGO Support Organisations (NGOSOs) and NGOs in Kazakstan and Kyrgyzstan providing training in organisational development, strategic planning, small enterprise development, PRA and other institutional support. We also fostered the beginning of co-ordination bodies in the four main republics through a regional workshop bringing together participants from Kyrgyzstan, Kazakstan, Uzbekistan and Tajikistan.

At the end of 1996, INTRAC's involvement in Central Asia was reviewed in the light of our experiences and lessons we had learned over the two years. The central theme of our findings at that time was that capacity-building efforts which focused exclusively on individual organisations would only allow limited development of the NGO sector while the overall 'environment' remained poor. Hence the approach taken was a broader 'institutional development of the sector as a whole' strategy rather than solely concentrating on the capacity-building of individual organisations within that sector.

This chapter reviews the first 18 months of the revised programme: it examines multiple strategic approaches to 'institutional development' dealing with changes that occur in the social structures that interact with NGOs, drawing out the lessons learned and how these feed into a modified programme for the next 18 months.

CONTEXT

At the end of 1991, the disintegration of the Soviet Union forced independence on the Central Asian states. Although independence has been widely accepted as inevitable and indeed, is now welcomed, there remain many bridges to be crossed.

NGO Sector: Ignored by Government and Donors

The NGO sector, in common with all sections of civil society[25], have been very marginalised in terms of lack of government support and resources. The legal framework for the NGO sector is still extremely poor and this has created conflict between both Government and NGOs and also amongst the NGOs themselves. In contrast, the business sector is far more acceptable to the nomenclaturist elite (bureaucratic decision-makers) and therefore legislative reform has been biased towards this sector. The international community is also far more

---

[25] defined as organised activities by groups or individuals either performing certain services or trying to influence and improve society as a whole, but are not part of government or business Clayton, 1996, *NGOs, Civil Society and the State*.

interested in seeing a free market take hold which has encouraged the government to place more emphasis on the development of the business sector.

The Role of NGOs Misunderstood

An issue that has continually overshadowed the sector has been the lack of understanding by government as to what constitutes an NGO. The relevant NGO laws inherited from the Soviet period effectively provide no clear definitions of what constitutes an NGO thus registration of NGOs is dependent on individual ministers' personal views (Garbutt and Sinclair 1998). In Uzbekistan the literal translation of non-government organisation is anti-government organisation, and because the NGO elite have had little exposure to NGOs outside Central Asia it is extremely difficult for them to eloquently dispel the myth amongst government officials that NGOs are *per se* against the government.

Throughout Central Asia there is a blurred distinction between NGOs and government. In both Kyrgyzstan and Uzbekistan, INTRAC found NGOs established by government officials who had been charged by the national government to act on social issues. One government official denoted the aspect of her job of working with unemployed women as being NGO work. She was genuinely confused about her role. More often than not, however, this blurring is brought about by the fact that NGOs attract funding that government does not.

As a result, governments throughout Central Asia view NGOs either as a threat to their own power base or as alternative service providers. In Kyrgyzstan relationships between government officials and NGOs function at a basic level only and when dissatisfied with a government service. The NGOs' response is usually to create an alternative rather than to improve upon whatever infrastructure already exists (Mellon 1998).

Ambiguous Role with Government

In the light of such confusion, NGOs have to play a very ambiguous role towards government. For example, NGO leaders in the capital cities are facing complex issues surrounding the position they hold and how much influence and contact they should have with government.

NGOs continually claim that governments take no responsibility for understanding the role NGOs could play in civil society. Unfortunately, the NGOs themselves do not recognise their own responsibility for helping governments understand their potential in building stronger communities. This creates serious problems for those NGOs who see their role inextricably linked to advocacy. This is partly because the concept of NGOs advocating on behalf of their target group is not strongly developed and NGOs have also not developed strong links with their target groups. Another possible reason for this is that NGOs are frequently dependent on local officials for their office space and other facilities, so creating a sense of powerlessness to affect change (Mellon 1998).

Most positive links between government and NGOs depend upon personal contacts or the positive attitude towards development by individual government officials. Governments in Central Asia are not monolithic entities and cannot be expected to act in a unified manner. This creates challenges for NGOs seeking to gain recognition with government. At the regional level NGO/government relationships depend very much on the local akimyat (mayor) and his/her understanding of NGO potential. At the national level NGOs in some sectors, such as health and social welfare and environment, have closer links with government. It is widely believed this is due to the amount of input into these sectors which external agencies provide. They are also sectors that do not threaten the power base of the government, unlike the human rights sector.

Weak on Performance

The NGO sector is still in a fledgling state throughout Central Asia, the oldest NGOs having developed since independence (other than the state run social groups now also registered as NGOs). It has thus proved difficult for the NGOs to show what they are capable of doing; they need more time to demonstrate how effective NGO programmes can be. They have considerable difficulty in placing their work in any kind of social and economic development context. There has also been a lack of systematic monitoring or periodic evaluation of activities led by NGOs, which has hampered their ability to prove to government that they are achieving what they say they can achieve. The NGO elite are therefore inclined to avoid meeting with government officials, particularly if they feel they will be questioned on their own performance.

NGOs Unsure of Own Role

Although the NGO sector began emerging in the late 1980s, exposure to peer sectors in other parts of the world has been and continues to be fairly limited, other than on environmental and health sector issues. One of the major concerns held by NGO personnel within all Central Asian states is a lack of information from outside that will help them better understand their role and influence within civil society. In the main, they see themselves as a link between the people and the state rather than as service providers, and this has implications for donors both in terms of funding and for support organisations, like INTRAC, in terms of approach. This fundamental difference means that the preconceived ideas we have from working with NGOs in other parts of the world do not necessarily hold true in Central Asia.

CONCEPT

NGO leaders in Central Asia have been extremely sensitive to Western experts transferring blueprints that have been developed in the west to Central Asia. 'Parachuting training' from Western experts is still all too common throughout the former Soviet Union. (Pratt and Goodhand 1996). It is the quality, rather than the quantity, of support provided to local NGOs by international agencies which will prove critical if it is to be effective. External support must be sensitive: many foreign agencies employ staff who have Russian language skills but often lack depth of experience and knowledge of development (Pratt and Goodhand 1996).

The present three-year programme managed by INTRAC promotes the development of the NGO sector by working with different levels of players who all affect the environment within which NGOs have to function. The overriding emphasis in supporting institutional development goes beyond simply improving the performance of individual NGOs *per se*. Although this is important, it focuses on what they do collectively in and for society. We are, therefore, expected to strengthen interactions within the NGO community as a way of reinforcing their position towards other institutional systems (Fowler, Campbell and Pratt 1992).

INTRAC began the 'Institutional Development of NGOs' programme by examining different strategies for working with the following groups of players.

- Communities
- Donors
- Government
- NGOSOs
- Co-ordination bodies
- NGOs

STRATEGIES

It was decided that INTRAC would attempt to work at multiple levels using several strategies and methodologies. Some of these strategies would be used at all levels, while others would be attempted at only one or two levels. These strategies and methods included:

- Facilitation of networking
- Providing advice and dialogue

- Organisational Development
- Training
- Exchange visits to both the UK and other countries
- Raising questions and providing information

Strategies Tried at Different Levels

	Comm-unity	Donors	Govt.	NGOSOs	Co-ordination Bodies	NGOs
Networking		Seminars Workshops		Seminars Workshops	Seminars Workshops	Seminars Workshops
Advice and dialogue	Dialogue	Legislation	Round-table meetings	Round-table	Meetings	Follow-up with NGOSOs
O.D.				Individual Team Intergroup Total orgn.	Individual Team Intergroup Total orgn.	Helping partners provide OD
Training	PRA	M and E, PRA ETSP TOT	Post PRA one day	M and E, PRA ETSP TOT	M and E PRA ETSP	PRA ETSP TOT
Exchange		Kyr-UK	Uzbek-UK Kyrg-UK	Kazak-UK Kyrg-UK Uzbek-UK Uzb-Kyrg Kyrg-Kaz Kaz-Kyr Kaz-Uz	Kyrg-Kaz	
Raising questions		Round-table Workshops	Meetings	Round-table Workshops Meetings	Round-table Workshop Meetings	with partners

Acronyms

ETSP – Education, Training and Support Programme
M&E – Monitoring and Evaluation
OD – Organisation Development

PRA – Participatory Rural Appraisal
TOT – Training of Trainers

Each of these strategies and methods of delivery is discussed below including the successes, challenges and the lessons learned.

Facilitation of Networking

INTRAC has maintained a facilitation role working with NGO support organisations and co-ordination bodies helping them with strategic planning, developing annual workplans and action learning techniques. In November 1997, INTRAC facilitated four seminars to examine the role of NGO support organisations. Two of these seminars were held for NGO support organisations in both Kazakstan and Kyrgyzstan and the other two were for the donors in both countries. It was decided to hold the seminars with peer groups only as INTRAC suspected that the NGO participants would be wary of speaking out in front of their donors. These seminars led to the establishment of quarterly round tables for the two groups in both Kazakstan and Kyrgyzstan, with INTRAC acting as secretary to all groups. The participants also felt that they were not ready to work together until they had reached consensus within their own peer group.

The donor meetings have been more successful than the NGOSO meetings mainly because the donor group feel more able to voice their concerns. Initially, a few of the larger, more influential donors sent quite junior staff to the meetings. However, as time has gone on, the donors have accepted the importance of the role these round-tables are taking. A major success that emerged from the donor group in Kazakstan was an initiative, in November 1998, whereby donors, NGOs and an American legal group met with government officials to discuss the way forward with appropriate legislation for non-governmental organisations. Although it is difficult for a small foreign NGO such as INTRAC to command the direct attention of government officials (maybe they should not), we have learned that there is a definite role for INTRAC as a result of facilitating quarterly round-tables. In continuing to lobby multinational and bilateral donors through these round-tables we are able to focus on NGO issues and encourage them to lobby government on behalf of NGOs.

The NGOSO round-table members in Kazakstan have not been as cohesive as in Kyrgyzstan. This is partly because they remain competitive with each other and do not recognise that working together will be beneficial to all concerned. INTRAC has, however, been able to raise the level of discussion at NGO support organisations' round-tables by focusing on NGO sector issues rather than those of individual NGOs. It is difficult for donors to play this role as often their own agenda colours discussion of the wider NGO issues. It is also possible for INTRAC, as an external organisation to help the NGOSOs analyse the problems they are facing. One of the main comments from the participants of these round tables is that 'INTRAC helps us to see things in a different way, which helps us to understand ourselves better.'

Providing Advice and Dialogue

The Project Manager has provided continual advisory support and maintained dialogue with various organisations including indigenous NGO support organisations, national co-ordination bodies, donor-initiated support projects and key individuals within the sector.

Indigenous NGO support organisations tend to ask for consultations when they are in a crisis or require help with an activity; they are less interested in continual input from INTRAC. This is possibly due to the number of years INTRAC provided intensive support before this programme commenced and the NGOSOs are better established than previously. There is a fine line between advisory support and interfering with the management of an organisation.

The newer donor-created support projects, however, have requested a more formal input, inviting INTRAC to strategic planning exercises and asking for advise on many issues, the combination of these becoming a form of accompaniment. Interestingly enough the indigenous organisations that INTRAC has been working with, as opposed to donor-created, appear to be doing better in establishing their credibility amongst NGOs and are more confident in their own decision-making processes. This almost certainly is due to the leadership being self-selected and committed to the role they are performing when supporting local NGOs. The donor-created support organisations are led by employees of the donors and therefore the executive decision-making powers remain in the hands of foreigners, thus undermining the confidence of the local leaders.

Once personal relationships have been established between INTRAC and local organisations they have allowed for disagreement while still continuing to work together. The importance of interpersonal relationships cannot be emphasised enough when working with Central Asian NGOs, particularly as the former USSR social structures were often solely dependant on who one knew rather than what one knew or one's status because of the bureaucratic nature of all structured systems.

It has proved to be essential that the staff who work alongside NGOs are of a senior level and have confidence in their own ability to advise. It is also important that what is being offered is what is needed (much more so than the traditional way of working with NGOs in the North who say, 'this is what we are going to do'). The indigenous NGOs are led by well-educated individuals who do not accept advice from people they think have little to offer.

Organisation Development

INTRAC has concentrated on a limited number of organisations when providing organisational development support. OD support is defined as a participatory and process-oriented development of clients' capabilities for future prob-

116

lem-solving (James 1998). There are an estimated 900 NGOs (Counterpart Consortium) throughout Central Asia: far too many for INTRAC to work with individually. Although there has been an increase in the number of organisations supported, the main issue concerning INTRAC is not so much how are we assisting NGOs to develop their organisations but what are they developing for.

The slow development of the NGO sector has been due partly to the lack of understanding on the part of foreign donors that the development of NGOs is inextricably linked to the economy within which NGOs operate. Donors often ask NGOs to provide long-term financial sustainability plans when the possibilities of creating internal resources are diminishing rapidly. The states of Central Asia were all heavily dependent on subsidies and transfers from Moscow and slow growth in the economy since the disintegration of the USSR has been reflected in the NGO sector. Unfortunately donors have concentrated on the establishment of, and to a certain extent the development of individual organisations rather than the NGO outputs and the role NGOs are playing within civil society.

Organisational change is influenced by many factors including the economic situation, the links with constituents, the environment and the individuals within the organisation. Many of the international donors who claim to be developing organisational change are only providing training to individuals within selected NGOs, while ignoring the other influences that lead to organisational change. There has been very little evidence of organisational change within NGOs throughout Central Asia.

INTRAC has provided a wide range of OD support to NGO support organisations in both Kazakstan and Kyrgyzstan. This has proved to be even more successful than the OD work with the co-ordination bodies. The main concern here is that some personnel from the support organisations also work for the co-ordination bodies. This has led to confusion in roles and a conflict of interest when making decisions on behalf of the co-ordination bodies. We are still talking of relatively new concepts of organisational structures, which has also helped increase the confusion.

As is often the case elsewhere, the level of governance in both the Kazak and Kyrgyz co-ordination bodies is poor, the membership is low and NGOs based outside the capital cities are suspicious of the leaders' motives. This has been particularly noticeable within the national co-ordination body in Kazakstan where the members have been working towards an agreed action plan, but continue to disagree on their role within the NGO community.

International organisations have a short-term view of their work and no real analysis or framework of their activities. This is often linked to the insecurity of their funding, which has led to short-term action planning. In other words the short-term perspective of donors working in Central Asia do not match the long-term prospect of transition. It is essential that we continue to keep a grasp on the larger vision otherwise we become embroiled in activities that have very little influence over the organisation as a whole or the longer-term Institutional Development.

Training

The INTRAC programme for introducing participatory training approaches, which was initiated before the present programme began, has continued to raise questions as to the value of introducing participatory methodologies when most organisations still lack a view of their roles as intermediaries working with 'communities' and how this role can be encapsulated into some form of project cycle or intervention. The Participatory Rural Appraisal (PRA) training introduced throughout Central Asia by INTRAC has been viewed by some as a means in itself rather than as a means to an end.

While the PRA concept was successfully taught to a group of participants, the assumption that they knew where this fitted into NGO activities was incorrect. What was lacking was an understanding of the value of PRA as a tool for influencing the NGO's purpose to link with its constituency's needs. The PRA programme has taught us that NGOs have little understanding of participatory approaches or development and that the next step is to introduce a more fundamental education, training and support programme which includes an understanding of development processes, practical knowledge of how to put ideas into practice examining why and how target groups influence policy and what mechanisms NGOs could use to make them operate more effectively.

While there are benefits to various teaching methodologies, there are cultural forces at play which international organisations must be aware of when designing training programmes or planning for participants to join training programmes in other countries. The PRA practitioners' training programme used methodologies, which challenged a complete world-view in which decisions came from above in a very structured and hierarchical system. It has become clear that we need to strike a balance between the benefits of less structured approaches and the cultural expectations of the participants. An example of this was when a director of a mature NGOSO in Kazakstan received language training in the UK at a Christian-based centre. The participant felt very isolated, as she was the only individual from a Muslim society and did not understand the use of Christian biblical language. The participant could have gained so much more if she had been placed in a non-sectarian training institution.

Exchange Visits to the UK and Other Countries

During the past 18 months, INTRAC has facilitated various visits to the UK by individual NGO personnel. These visits included five senior NGOSO people to an international NGOSO conference where participants were able to meet and work with NGOSO people from not only Northern and Southern NGOs but also other eastern NGOSOs from Russia and the Ukraine. At the conference many discussions were held around defining the role of NGOSOs and the added value they provide to the development NGO sector. Exchange visits have a valuable place in the Central Asia NGO sector. However, there is limited value if the participants have not been prepared fully and if the environment they return to is moving in a different direction and is led by different actors.

The exchange visits have shown that the participants who have visited other countries are beginning to use a common language with NGOs in other parts of the world. This has helped them to articulate their needs more clearly.

Three members of the Kyrgyz Forum of Women's NGOs visited the UK to work with INTRAC trainers and visited other NGOs who are involved in women's issues in the UK. The participants were able to see different training techniques directly and increase the number of materials for their resource centre. They were also exposed to UK-based NGOs who use different methods of supporting NGOs other than those used by INTRAC.

Senior staff of an NGOSO based in Kyrgyzstan participated in an exchange visit to Mongolia where they were able to see first hand the use of PRA methodologies in practice. This exchange indicated that the NGOs need to meet with counterparts in other areas of the world to help them understand that they are not alone in the problems they face.

The participants have shown that the closed mind set expected of former Soviet Union states is not as closed as was initially thought and that they are willing to learn from anyone if the message is clear. This also shows that after a period of a number of years' exposure, experience has widened expectations and increased openness.

Raising Questions

During the past 18 months several INTRAC internal papers have been used in Central Asia to open discussions and debates by attempting to raise some of the issues that have been underlying problems faced by the NGO sector.

One of the major aims has been to help the organisations to examine their roles and limitations and begin the process of understanding the level of influence they have in the NGO sector. In October 1998 a discussion paper on NGO support organisations was prepared and presented to four seminars attended by NGOSOs, donors and international NGOs. The major aim of the seminars was to help the participants examine issues surrounding external forces on the NGO sector, NGOSOs as donors and the accountability of NGOSOs. The final outcome of the seminars is four round-tables examining the problems facing NGOs in Kyrgyzstan and Kazakstan held on a quarterly basis. The four groups also realised that they must work harder at influencing government and also spent quite some time considering the institutionalisation of NGO support.

Four NGO mapping reports have been completed in Kyrgyzstan, Kazakstan, Uzbekistan and Turkmenistan. The reports take into account not only where the NGOs are physically based but also what they are doing, what the government links are like and what constituency they are working with. The feedback of these reports will be essential in assisting the NGOs, donors and government to understand their roles and the roles of the other players who affect the sector. INTRAC will continue to stimulate debate around the roles of NGOs and the responsibilities they must take in the development of the non-profit sector. While, the NGOs are all aware of their own positions within the NGO sector, they are still unaware of their potential to influence the growth of the whole of civil society.

CONCLUSION

Our multilevel intervention means that we have had to remain flexible at all times: knowing when to provide help and when to hold back. The nature of the programme means we have to keep a wide perspective at all times rather than focusing on project activities. We have also needed to remain aware of the different actors and the multiplicity of stakeholders who come to the fore, having a particular role to play at different times.

We have to keep all options open and be able to step in when the opportunity presents itself, for example linking with an international agency such as the UNDP-initiated NGO Resource Centre where we have provided accompaniment support to the newly appointed staff, while at the same time assisting a women's NGO forum to establish itself and begin to understand its role within the NGO sector. The environment within transitional countries is moving rapidly and changing direction continually. It is essential that any organisation providing institutional capacity-building support is able to change and grow as rapidly as the partners with whom it works.

If donors were to consider sectoral programme approaches rather than NGO project approaches, the blurring between NGOs and government could be minimised. To date donors have tended to see only the immediate problem of delivering services rather than developing or capacity-building local groups. They have, therefore, employed UN volunteers or Peace Corps volunteers, so slowing down the process of indigenous capacity-building.

INTRAC plans to employ a community development adviser to address issues surrounding the NGOs working within one sector and to examine ways of bridging the gap between government, NGOs and the community they are both targeting. This approach will also examine how links between the different players can minimise tensions and create more effective working environments for all involved. We believe that the information gathered and then disseminated will assist NGOs in other sectors to a better understanding of their role in developing the capacity of communities to solve their own problems and thus increase the capacity of NGOs within civil society.

In terms of impact so far, the programme has been too diverse and widely spread to measure impact easily, but the recent evaluation of the programme by HIVOS and NOVIB made some attempt. They comment on results to date and short term impact:

'Measuring results of a programme such as INTRAC's is highly complex since there are no immediate and easily 'measurable' indicators such as blatant success stories or achievements depending solely on INTRAC activities. In the evaluation two main indicators were considered to assess results and impact. One was the responses, reactions and analysis of INTRAC partners to the programme and the second was an attempt to measure the 'suitability' of INTRAC strategies against the context with its external constraints and opportunities. As far as the first indicator is concerned, responses to the INTRAC programme were positive and all INTRAC primary partners (NGOSOs and NGOs) expressed directly and indirectly the impact and benefits they had obtained through different types of work and interaction with INTRAC.

Under the second category, a multiplicity of factors were considered. One of the most evident conclusions was that NGOs who were INTRAC partners showed a stronger degree of internal development and better understanding of development issues than non-partner NGOs. This is inevitably a partial indicator since it is difficult to determine to what extent the strength of an organisation depends solely on the organisation itself or on INTRAC's inputs. Nevertheless the correlation exists and the evaluators believe it to be significant. In terms of NGO organisational capacity, accountability and performance much ground has been covered since the start of the INTRAC programme. Given the lack of prolonged experience and constraints characterising the NGO sector, INTRAC activities and strategies have contributed to the development and first signs in strengthening of a group of key-player NGOs and NGOSOs.

Part Five

Power and Partnership

Chapter 8

Conclusion
Power and Partnership

The Introduction to this book highlighted a number of current issues in the field of NGO capacity-building relating to 'what is capacity-building'. The bulk of the publication then examined a number of different capacity-building interventions. From these cases and the synthesis chapter from IFCB there are a number of insights and implications arising, not from desk-bound theories, but from the actual practice of NGO capacity-building.

In this concluding chapter we shall deal with:

1. the capacity-building **needs** identified by the Southern NGOs themselves;
2. the impact of the **context** on the capacity-building intervention;
3. the **nature** of the capacity-building practised – the levels and areas of intervention;
4. the **principles of good practice** for capacity-building interventions;
5. the links between capacity-building and **programme impact** on beneficiaries;
6. the pervasive influence of **power** in capacity-building; and
7. the implications for **partnerships** in capacity-building.

CAPACITY-BUILDING NEEDS AND PRIORITIES

The IFCB chapter provides some fascinating and important insights, particularly from the South, in terms of the perceived capacity-building priorities. One of the obvious, but critical, findings of the IFCB study is that different stakeholders identify different capacity-building needs of Southern NGOs. In the past capacity-building needs have largely been defined by the funders rather than the recipients of capacity-building. Consequently, 'many Southern NGOs see the past emphasis on training for accounting and financial management as a response to Northern concerns with accountability for resources they contribute, rather than an effort to build capacities needed to implement SNGO missions or to promote sustainable local development'. Identification of capacity-building needs by someone other than the client, has meant that the ensuing interventions have not been owned by those they were meant to assist, and their impact has therefore been undermined.

The IFCB report differentiates between individual capacities; organisational capacities; and capacities for external relations. At the level of **individual** capacities Southern NGOs, particularly in South Asia and Southern and Eastern Africa, identified leadership development as a top priority. Such programmes were viewed as essential to both improve existing NGO leadership and to enable succession to 'second generation' leaders. Southern NGOs generally rated individual capacity-building as being more important than did Northern NGOs or donors.

The area of **organisational capacity-building** was also emphasised by Southern NGOs with *planning and strategic management* rated as high priority by every region. *Organisation renewal and development* and *programme design and management* were also accorded high priority by most regions. Another key element of organisational capacity emphasised by the survey is the capacity for *resource mobilisation.* Not surprisingly, while donors and Northern NGOs are more concerned with promoting local resource mobilisation, the Southern respondents were more keen to improve the quality of donor funding.

The issue of Southern NGO capacity for **external relations**, especially with governments and other civil society actors, was given very high priority by Northern NGOs and donors. Southern NGOs also give high priority to building capacity for policy analysis and advocacy and to networking with other NGOs. SNGOs did not, however, rate collaborating with business as a high priority, except in Latin America.

THE INFLUENCE OF CONTEXT

The case studies presented all clearly point to the profound and far-reaching influence which the different contexts had in determining:

- the nature of the internal capacity-building needs;
- the appropriateness of different capacity-building interventions; and
- the nature of the impact of the capacity-building programme.

The context in which NGOs are working is changing rapidly. NGOs are being asked to do more and do it better in the wake of massive global, regional and national changes in the economic, social, political and technological spheres. The reality for most NGOs is that due to globalisation, the environment in which they operate is increasingly complex and unpredictable. These changes have had a considerable impact on the NGO sector whether in terms of funding flows or stakeholder demands and needs. As a result, 'the importance of learning as a key organisational capacity has become increasingly apparent in the changing, unpredictable economic and political environment of the 1990s' according to Hailey[26]. He goes on to note that, 'the survival and success of any organisation operating in any turbulent environment is dependent, as Reg Revans (one of the early pioneers of action learning) noted, on its rate of learning being 'equal to or greater than the rate of change in its environment'. As Alan Fowler (1997) so succinctly commented, unless NGOs learn, 'they are destined for insignificance'. The changing NGO context has had a major influence on capacity-building being on the agenda in the first place. Reading the case studies, the influence of the external environment is clear. For example, one trigger for the launch of the Agenda for Action in Mozambique was the government regulation of international NGOs in 1998. Similarly, it is the changing context in which churches operate and are funded in Africa which provides the rationale for much of CORAT's work. Obviously, too, the break up of the former Soviet Union was the trigger for the emergence of the NGO sector in Central Asia and therefore the corresponding NGO capacity-building programme.

The cases also show that **the context affected the nature of the capacity-building need**. The regional studies conducted by the IFCB, show how different contexts produce different priority areas. In South Asia, respondents highlighted that different countries had different capacity-building needs at different times. The CDS/ CRDT case illustrates how the Arab context had a pervasive influence on the nature of the capacity-building needs in gender. The Soviet cultural legacy of centralised bureaucracy in Central Asia was also seen to be critical in determining the capacity-building needs in that area. Similarly in Malawi, it is the context of 30 years of autocratic rule which has made leadership development the priority NGO capacity-building need.[27]

As well as having a profound effect on determining the capacity-building need, it was clearly seen that **the context has a considerable influence on the nature of the resulting capacity-building interventions**. The context partly determined which capacity-building methodology was appropriate as well as influencing the details of those interventions. For example, the CORAT leader-

[26] John Hailey – unpublished paper given at conference, 'Control and Consent: Promoting Learning in NGOs'.
[27] R. James, 1999, 'Up Close and Personal'.

ship training case described the use of biblical stories to contextualise the training; in OD in Malawi local proverbs are often used; and in Central Asia the design of the training interventions had to take cognisance of the lack of experience of more participative training techniques. According to the IFCB report, 'to become effective and appropriate to local circumstances, programmes may have to be extensively 'contextualised' to fit the cultural expectations, political contexts, economic circumstances and historical development of Southern civil societies and NGO communities'.

Lastly, the context also has a deep influence on the nature of the impact of the capacity-building programme. To a large degree this reflects the ubiquitous development dilemma, that if you target the 'poorest of the poor' you will usually get less measurable impact, while if you target better-off individuals, group, regions, countries with more dynamic economies then the programmes have 'better results'. Similarly, with capacity-building programmes, one may see more measurable changes in the stronger NGOs than the weaker ones. There seems to be some trade-off between the need for capacity-building on the one hand and the impact of a capacity-building programme on the other. The catch-22 is that the greater the NGOs' need for capacity-building the more these very weaknesses will constrain the impact of the capacity-building.

THE NATURE OF CAPACITY-BUILDING IN PRACTICE

While theoretical notions of capacity-building remain slippery, contentious and vague, the chapters presented here do shed very useful and pragmatic light on what is understood by capacity-building in practice.

The examples of capacity-building described a wide **variety of approaches** (including training, OD consultancies, inter-organisational linkages, exchange visits and networking), at a **variety of levels** (such as individual, organisational or societal) and addressed a wide **variety of issues** (programme, organisational and relational). The IFCB report indicated that 'training individuals is an important component of capacity-building for Southern NGOs, but it is only one element of what could be a much broader concept that includes a wide variety of interventions that can strengthen Southern NGO roles in development - from team-building with key leadership groups, to organisation design and development consultations, to network building and support programmes, to enhancing legal frameworks and tax policies that foster or inhibit the development of NGOs as a sector'.

The cases reinforce the definition outlined in the introduction that 'capacity-building is an ongoing process – a conscious intervention to help people, organisations and societies improve and adapt to changes around them.

Performance and improvements are taken in the light of the mission, objectives, context, resources and sustainability.'

Before examining the specific capacity-building interventions, it is interesting to note that all the contributors studiously avoided embroiling themselves in the debate over whether capacity-building should be better termed capacity-enhancement or capacity-strengthening or capacity-development. One conclusion from this is that for the more 'activist' capacity-building practitioners this debate is proving rather sterile and academic. Rather than spend too much time discussing semantics, they prefer to just get on with capacity-building and use whatever words are generally accepted.

Furthermore, the issue of whether capacity-building is an internal or external intervention was also not directly addressed by the cases, though they were all external interventions. One presentation at the conference, however, which is not able to be included in this publication for copyright reasons, did indirectly address this theme. John Hailey's research with a cross-section of nine leading South Asian NGOs (including BRAC, Proshika, AKRSP and BAIF) concluded that learning (which he described as synonymous with capacity-building) 'is a dynamic process which integrates informal processes with more formal structures and systems'. Although they are not entirely synonymous, external interventions are largely 'formal' learning processes and internal interventions can be both, though tend to be more on the 'informal side'. Capacity-building is therefore seen as both an external and an internal intervention. Interestingly he found that the balance between the informal and the formal learning shifted over time from informal to more formal methods as the evidence suggested that, as organisations grow, informal processes are not able to generate the diversity of learning needed by larger, more complex organisations.

Levels of Intervention
The actual examples of capacity-building programmes point to a variety of approaches to capacity-building at a variety of levels.

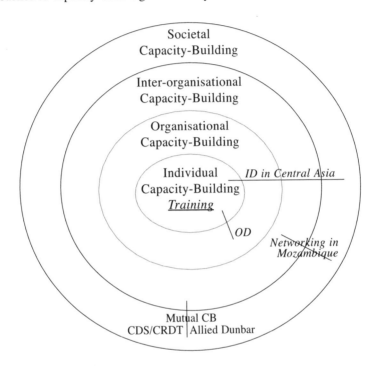

The above model shows the different levels at which the various case studies focused. This demonstrates that there are a number of **different strategic choices** for NGO capacity-building programmes. The CORAT case described a leadership training intervention which was focused exclusively at an individual level (though with links to other levels). The OD chapter illustrates interventions with an 'organisational capacity-building' focus, while the examples with CDS/CRDT and Opportunity International and Allied Dunbar reveal more of an inter-organisational capacity-building strategy. The'Agenda for Action for Children' case from Mozambique describes an intervention with a fairly exclusive focus on 'societal' capacity-building. In contrast the capacity-building programme from Central Asia chose to aim to build capacity concurrently at all levels. The Central Asia programme describes 'working at multiple levels (communities, donors, governments, NGOSOs, co-ordination bodies and NGOs)'.

The cases clearly demonstrate, too, that these levels are **highly permeable** membranes and that interventions at one level have implications at other levels.

The CORAT leadership training programme is consciously being reinforced by OD work with many of the participating leaders' organisations. Similarly OD work with organisations is also increasingly recognising that organisation-wide interventions which do not also recognise the very personal and individual nature of organisational change are doomed to fail. While it is easy to talk in fairly impersonal terms about the need for leadership commitment to organisational change, experience suggests that in fact what is often needed for any organisational change is 'leadership commitment to their own *personal* change'[28] as it is their inner attitudes and assumptions which shape the organisation's culture and strategy (particularly in younger organisations). According to Allan Kaplan of CDRA in South Africa 'if leadership cannot shift then no organisational processes can succeed.'[29] . The CORAT leadership programme is based on the notion that 'if we develop effective leaders then there is a chance to develop effective organisations'. The line then between individual change at a leadership level and organisational change may be often more conceptual than actual.

In addition, the whole aim of organisational capacity-building programmes is that they do have an impact outside the organisation – on the outer layers – in terms of changes in beneficiary (society) lives as well as changed relations with other organisations such as donors. Indeed, most capacity-building programmes are developed on the assumption that there is a direct relationship between organisational change and impact at societal level.

In any capacity-building programme strategic choices must be made as to which level or levels will be the entry point and which will be the main areas of focus. These strategic choices in turn raise an important question: does the programme have to try and build capacity at all levels at the same time (a holistic and integrated approach) or does it need to focus capacity-building energies and resources on the one (or two) critical level(s) and aim for indirect change at other levels? Just as the cases illustrate, different organisations will have different answers to this inherent strategic dilemma in different contexts. Whatever choice is made it should be based on a thorough assessment of the particular situation and organisations involved.

[28] R. James, 1999, 'Up Close and Personal'.
[29] P. Crockett, 1996, 'OD Useful in Changing Times: Interview with Allan Kaplan'.

Different Areas of Intervention:
The cases also display marked differences in their areas of capacity-building emphasis. Using the INTRAC clover leaf model described in the introduction:

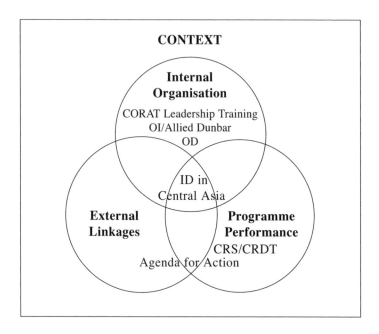

CONTEXT

Internal Organisation
CORAT Leadership Training
OI/Allied Dunbar
OD

ID in Central Asia

External Linkages

Programme Performance
CRS/CRDT

Agenda for Action

Some of the cases focused their interventions in the programme area. The CDS/CRDT case study largely described work between two organisations in a common 'programme' area – namely gender training. The Mozambique case was in the particular programme area of child rights.

Other cases took more of an organisational focus, such as CORAT's work with leadership, the OD examples and 'mutual capacity-building' cases.

The Mozambique case also used external relations as its main way of achieving its programme goal. The Central Asia case shows a variety of interventions in different areas with programme-related PRA training and the employment of a community development adviser as well as OD interventions with specific organisations and facilitation work bringing networks of NGO support organisations and co-ordination bodies as well as donors together.

Again we see that capacity-building offers a number of different potential focus areas. What is also clear is that these focus areas are sometimes entry points to working in other areas too. As with the concentric circles model, the lines between the different areas become very blurred. For example, working with organisations on improving their gender training programme delivery brings into very sharp relief internal gender issues within the training providers' organisations themselves. Similarly many OD interventions with NGOs are in fact initiated through 'programme' evaluations. In addition, the Mozambican case showed that in order to achieve an impact on a programme area like 'child rights' an approach which focused largely on improving the external relations between organisations was used.

An unpublished paper presented by Gavin Andersson[30] at the conference explored the theory of 'unbounded organisations' that emphasised the importance of looking systematically at the 'external relations' element. He comments:

> Organisational theory invariably, and naturally, focuses more on individual enterprises than the relationships between them. As the complexity of the development task is increasingly recognised, the limitations of individual organisations in achieving that task in isolation are also increasingly apparent. The prerequisite is to work coherently and co-operatively within a whole system of diverse organisations in order to achieve the common goal.

The old capacity-building debate about whether capacity-building should be programme (technical)-focused or organisationally-focused seems to have moved on. The consensus emerging from the practice of capacity-building is that it is not a question of either-or, but both-and; and while at it one must include the external relations dimension as well. It appears that whether a capacity-building intervention is being made at the organisational level, or in the programme area, it is very important to relate (though not necessarily implement) that intervention to all the areas. So, for example, technical programme-related interventions need to understand the internal organisational implications and the required external relations dynamics. By the same token, organisational interventions must beware of becoming too introspective and maintain the emphasis on programme impact at beneficiary level as well as the implications for external relations.

GOOD PRACTICE IN CAPACITY-BUILDING

As with other studies of capacity-building, all these cases reaffirm the fundamental pre-requisite for any capacity-building to succeed – it must be **owned**

---

[30] Gavin Andersson – unpublished paper given at conference, 'Unbounded organisation: de morais and Social Change'.

and driven by the organisation on the receiving end. While there needs to be a critical mass of staff support, the capacity-building programme must also have top leadership drive. Acquiescence to capacity-building by the NGO generally or the leadership specifically is not enough. This provides a fundamental challenge to other stakeholders (such as INGO or official donors) who wish to be involved in supporting capacity-building. They have to support a process which, first and foremost, must be owned by someone else and therefore cannot by definition be 'theirs'. While addressing their own back-donors' concerns for accountability they have to recognise that to achieve genuine impact they must relinquish control of the capacity-building process at the very start. If they continue to dominate the identification of capacity-building needs on behalf of their 'partners', the impact of such programmes will continue to be patchy. As the IFCB report bluntly states, 'when capacity is seen as essential, individuals, groups and organisations often invest much time, energy and talent to build it. The same actors may prove very slow learners if the capacities are perceived to be imposed in response to someone else's agenda'. One key element of this 'ownership' that was highlighted by the OD chapter is the usual need for the NGO to experience some pain, a sense of urgency, and a recognition that the status quo is not an acceptable solution for the future. In Mozambique, this sense of **urgency** was achieved in the first workshop through participants contemplating 'the human cost of not fulfilling children's rights'.

Another factor that emerged from a number of the cases is that the different stakeholders need to play **different roles** in the process. There were three major stakeholders in most of the capacity-building interventions described, namely the client, the capacity-building provider and the donor. Each stakeholder had a different role in the process and it was important to **clarify these different roles** and keep to boundaries. The Mozambican case notes that success can be attributed partly to 'clear institutional arrangements'. It is also interesting to note the changing roles of some actors, such as CDS in the linkage programme. CDS/CRDT describe 'an iterative process of redesign and renegotiation'. One boundary which was not crossed, however, was that of mixing funding and capacity-building. In all of the examples described the **direct providers of capacity-building did not also provide funds** to the clients. One of the most obvious dangers in many capacity-building processes is the blurring of the distinction between the donor and the capacity-building provider which tends to manipulate or undermine the process in negative ways which will be discussed in more detail further on.

As well as having clear roles, the various stakeholders must respect and value the different contributions of other stakeholders if capacity-building is to succeed according to both the Mozambican Agenda for Action case and CDS/CRDT linkage example. NGOs are not islands, but open systems, and so it is often important to involve a variety of stakeholders in the capacity-building processes.

It is clear from the description of all of the capacity-building examples that **generous and 'hands-off' donors** were involved. Although not directly stated, but obvious from the text, the interventions described required significant investment over a period of time. CORAT's leadership development programme is spread over more than one year; the OD work mentioned in the chapter is still ongoing after 18 months; the CDS/CRDT linkage took place over six years and similarly the Central Asia ID programme is now in its sixth year. Commitment from donors to long-term solutions was an essential element of the capacity-building programmes.

In terms of the actual design of the capacity-building programmes there are a number of good practice learnings:

Follow-Through

Most of the case studies also emphasise the fact that capacity-building is an ongoing process, not a one-off event. As a result, whether it is training, OD, linkages or even an institutional development programme, they all need significant time commitment to succeed. Follow-through is not an optional extra after the intervention, but an integral part of the intervention itself.

Participatory Processes

The different capacity-building interventions also emphasised the need for capacity-building processes to be participatory irrespective of whether they were training, OD, linkages or networking. A highly practical, 'learning through experience' approach to capacity-building permeated all the cases.

Mixture of Methodologies

As has been stated already, the recognition of the multiple levels of capacity-building and the usefulness of a variety of change strategies were also identified by the cases as a key factor in success. So for example the CORAT leadership training benefited through its emphasis on training teams from organisations and complementing training with organisation-wide interventions. Similarly the OD interventions required an emphasis on individual change in order to achieve organisational change.

Incentives

A controversial factor rarely addressed in capacity-building but mentioned at the conference is the benefit of introducing some incentives to the capacity-building process both for the recipients and the providers based on measures of performance (not just attendance). For providers of capacity-building, one of the key success factors in training (from Hailey's research) was the introduction of post-training financial incentives whereby calculation of the trainer's salary 'was based on the response of 10% of those trained to 10 standard questions'.

Other

Other common factors contributing to success include a **thorough analysis** of the real capacity-building need; the **flexibility** of the capacity-building programmes enabling them to change over time as new needs emerge (for example the CDS/CRDT MOU was rewritten twice during the programme); and the importance of seeing organisations and change as **highly political entities and processes** (as illustrated by a number of the cases and examined in detail below).

THE LINKS BETWEEN CAPACITY-BUILDING AND IMPACT

A key question to ask in any capacity-building programme is: 'capacity-building for what?'. What is the ultimate goal to be achieved? As capacity-building has shifted away from an exclusive focus on programmes and technical issues towards investing in organisations, so there has been a rising concern that capacity-building is being pursued and funded as an end in itself. There is a worry that all the resources invested in capacity-building have not trickled-down to programme impact for the ultimate beneficiaries. This leads to the argument that capacity-building programmes should be directed more at community groups than the more 'unsustainable' NGO intermediaries.

The cases presented, while noting the need for 'an external expression of their learning' (CDS/CRDT) furnished very limited evidence of impact at the level of beneficiaries. This is due largely to the severe methodological problems associated with such an exercise. The INTRAC case from Central Asia benefited from an external evaluation which pointed out that 'measuring results of a programme such as INTRAC's is highly complex since there are no immediate and easily "measurable" indicators such as blatant success stories or achievements depending solely on INTRAC activities'. There are some major issues to consider which may reduce the certainty of any judgement, but do not negate the need to try. First, there are problems associated with the **'counter-factual'** – divining what would have happened without the capacity-building programme. As each organisation is unique, control groups are very difficult. Second, there are problems of **attribution** – to what extent can any change be attributed specifically to the capacity-building programme? Organisations are notoriously 'noisy', complex environments making it very difficult to try and isolate the particular effects of different factors on a process of change. For example, to what extent can a shift in an organisation's strategy be attributed to a capacity-building intervention or to the arrival of a new senior staff member or to new donor funding? Third, the impact of the capacity-building programme becomes more **indirect and diffuse** as it permeates the different levels. To what extent is it therefore really possible to evaluate the impact of a leadership counselling programme, by interviewing the ultimate beneficiaries in the communities? They are highly unlikely to have seen any direct change, but that does not mean that it has not occurred. Fourth, there is the problem of **time-scale** – when will the real impact of a capacity-building programme be seen – in one year, five years, ten years or thirty years? Whatever time-scale is chosen will be arbitrary to some extent.

Despite these methodological problems, NGOs cannot ignore the question, 'Capacity-building for what?' and need to work on ways to identify the impact of organisational capacity-building at community level. Some agencies are beginning to make attempts to get to grips with this issue. A number of donors and Northern NGOs have approached INTRAC to assist their developing appropriate methodologies for measuring the impact of their capacity-building programmes. UNICEF, in particular, is in the process of developing a major manual for field staff highlighting guiding principles and describing a number of participative tools.

At the same time, interested parties must recognise the inherent methodological constraints which will prevent anything more than a 'rough idea' of impact. To some extent, those working from an organisational capacity-building perspective have to assume that a more effective organisation will have a greater impact. Some evidence does exist indicating a link between improved internal organisation and programme impact (James 1998). Certainly an organisation which is facing severe internal issues is likely to divert attention from its programme work with beneficiaries to internal wranglings and conflicts. In order to act in capacity-building and development generally, certain assumptions will always have to be made. What is important is that these assumptions are made explicit – 'we are assuming that stronger NGOs will have greater impact in communities' – and that periodically some attempt is made to see whether they do in fact hold true.

Perhaps more importantly in capacity-building then is the need to demonstrate measurable impact at least in terms of **organisational change**. The cases presented do give some evidence for this. For example in Central Asia one of the most evident conclusions of an evaluation was that NGOs who were INTRAC partners showed a stronger degree of internal development and a better understanding of development issues than non-partner NGOs. The LOMADEF OD case also points to changes resulting from the capacity-building intervention such as developing a clear mission and strategy shared by the whole organisation, a decentralisation of power and decision-making, and a growth in size. Furthermore, the funding of LOMADEF by a donor after the OD intervention demonstrates that some changes were evident to others. The CDS/CRDT case pointed to attitude-based changes in the organisations regarding gender equity, and training and consultancy practice. Increased skills in preparation, delivery, documentation and evaluation of training were also the result of the capacity-building programme as well as various written manuals, modules, checklists and papers.

The cases also provide evidence that clients were satisfied with the capacity-building interventions. For example, positive **evaluations of capacity-building inputs** was mentioned by the CORAT training case and the INTRAC ID programme in Central Asia. More telling is the **increased demand for capacity-building services**. On the assumption that clients will not waste time and money on capacity-building if it has not proved effective in the past, the increased demand for capacity-building services and repeat purchase of capacity-building would indicate that the capacity-building had had some impact. For example, the CORAT clients have returned for additional training as well as inviting CORAT to do consultancy work with them and CABUNGO is being asked to continue and develop their support for LOMADEF. CDS/CRDT also mentioned increased demand for work being a key output of the capacity-building.

POWER AND CAPACITY-BUILDING

While power and capacity-building are rarely mentioned in the same breath, the cases reveal what a **potent, pervasive and often perverse impact power has on capacity-building programmes**. This power can be examined at a micro-level (within organisations) or at a macro-level (between organisations).

Power within Organisations

Within an organisation, power dynamics often ultimately determine whether the capacity-building interventions will have impact. One of the key success factors emerging from the cases, particularly the OD chapter was the importance of top management, not merely accepting change, but driving change. For capacity-building programmes to work, it is clear that key power people must support the initiative. There are numerous examples of informal and formal power structures causing severe blocks to change processes which may undermine some aspect of their power, whether it be their perceived expertise, their status or their control over resources.

Hailey's unpublished paper entitled 'Control or Consent' outlines the debate

136

over whether organisational change is best managed through control or consent and quotes Child's view that training and staff development are part of a strategy to control the culture. Other writers such as McKendall see OD as a sophisticated form of managerial manipulation for inducing compliance and uniformity into the organisation. In looking at any capacity-building interventions it is important to analyse 'whose interests is this serving?' both outside and inside the organisation. The formal and the informal dimensions of power (including the negative power of veto, obstruction or non-co-operation from supposedly weaker players) need to be understood. Capacity-building is not quite as pure and value-free as many would have us believe. The power dynamics within organisations must be thoroughly understood and analysed if change is to occur.

Power Dynamics between Organisations

The importance of understanding the power dynamics between organisations involved in capacity-building is largely ignored by the 'powerful' NNGOs and donors. Many Northern NGOs would like to ignore the power that control over resources ultimately gives them and prefer to talk the language of partnership (until something goes wrong). Southern NGOs are much more keenly aware of such power issues. The IFCB study from South Asian NGOs signalled the pervasive influence of power in capacity-building by entitling their whole report, 'Politics of Capacity-Building' and the two IFCB consultations in Africa actually 'ignored issues of North-South co-operation because of widespread belief they would not have any impact'. In addition, the case studies presented also reveal that effective capacity-building programmes must integrate a political perspective on a number of levels.

Capacity-building sounds a very neutral, even positive term and one that is impossible to disagree with. This is an illusion. Capacity-building reinforces or undermines existing power dynamics. On a macro-level, one must ask, whose interest is the capacity-building programme serving? Is the capacity-building programme merely to make SNGOs better recipients of aid and ensure that the implementation of the structural adjustment programmes go more smoothly? The IFCB work was a systematic attempt to articulate capacity-building from the South. In the past it has often been the Northern agencies defining the capacity-building needs of the South and not surprisingly these 'Southern needs' have focused on Northern needs for good monitoring and evaluation information and financial and narrative reporting. According to the IFCB survey, Southern NGOs see Northern practice as far behind its rhetoric in capacity-building; the services offered often seem tailored to the interest and needs of Northern providers rather than Southern recipients. So it is capacity-building in the interest of the powerful.

The Self-Interest of Capacity-Building

There is a self-interested side to capacity-building. Given the high cost of most capacity-building (and best practice points to even higher investment needed) it will have to be subsidised from the outside to a degree (notwithstanding the need for as much cost recovery as possible). Those outsiders who are needed to subsidise capacity-building programmes will necessarily have their own interests and agendas. The capacity-building programme in the Mozambican case study arose out of a need for Northern NGOs to redefine their role in the light of greater public scrutiny and legislation. This self-interest is legitimate and not morally reprehensible as has often been the unwritten assumption particularly amongst Northern NGOs. The tendency is for Northerners to deny anything but altruistic motives with the result that self-interests have been submerged, but not eliminated. To some degree there will always be self-centred agendas. What is important is to recognise and not hide that self-interest. As the Allied Dunbar/ZFS case shows, an honest acceptance of self-interest provides a stable framework for capacity-building. This allows people to accept it and work constructively with it. When these interests are shrouded by nice rhetoric then the ground begins to shift beneath your feet.

Power Issues Undermining the Effectiveness of Capacity-Building

Interestingly most of the cases presented involve capacity-building providers who do not have any direct funding relationship with the beneficiaries. This came out as a key factor for success in the linkage programme and is a usual criterion for good practice in OD. Once funding becomes involved then the capacity-building programme gets hopelessly confused as a 'funding hoop' and cosmetic changes to secure funding are introduced. Authentic change remains as elusive as ever. Control over resources is one of the most potent and basic sources of power, especially in the NGO world. As the IFCB report concluded: 'it is easy for donors, seen by recipients as very powerful in their ability to control essential resources, to remain unaware of how much communications can be distorted by real or perceived power asymmetries. Potential beneficiaries of capacity-building programmes may be reluctant to explain what kinds of programmes are really needed for fear they will be seen as unworthy of future support.'

Power dynamics between organisations also affect the efficacy of capacity-building programmes. Many Northern agencies want to build the capacity of partners, but not give the partners any room to implement that capacity. The IFCB report warned that if capacity-building initiatives embody or reinforce Northern dominance and Southern dependence, then programme impacts are likely to be counter-productive. NNGO intentions and rhetoric are about relinquishing control, but in reality they find it extremely hard to let go. Capacity-building is inextricably linked to control and Northern agencies cannot hope to build capacity while at the same time retaining 'control'. The critical question in capacity-building is whether or not **power is a zero-sum or positive sum game**. If capacity-building programmes really 'empower' Southern NGOs then does this add to the overall sum of power or does the power of the Northern donor consequently reduce by the same amount? Sometimes Northern NGOs talk as if they believe power to be a positive sum game, but act as if it is zero-sum.

The case where outside interests may have been least controlling was that of Allied Dunbar. They were very open about their interest in the programme (for their staff development) and were fortunate that this programme was fairly peripheral to their main activity (commercial insurance). It was easier for Allied Dunbar/ZFS to relinquish because this capacity-building programme was only a minor part of their overall internal HRD programme not a key part of their operations strategy as is the case with most NGOs.

While power differences are inevitable among stakeholders in many capacity-building programmes, the pervasive effects of such differences must first be recognised and understood before they can be effectively managed. Taking up an ostrich-like pose and pretending that they do not exist either between organisations or within organisations serves only to exacerbate the power dynamics and probably undermine the impact of any capacity-building programme. If awareness of these issues is absent, the tendency is for the powerful to inadvertently manipulate capacity-building programmes to their ends and thereby remove ownership from the supposed beneficiary.

PARTNERSHIP IN CAPACITY-BUILDING

The cases clearly demonstrate another key conclusion - that authentic capacity-building is at least two-way. The description of an 'aid chain' is an increasingly common way of seeing how aid moves from one set of people in the North, through Northern governments to multilaterals and Northern NGOs; to Southern NGOs and then reaching Southern community groups. For development aid to go from people to people, it has to travel along a whole chain. The tendency is to define the capacity-building needs at the level of the chain 'below' one. Consequently, official donors have questioned the value added by Northern NGOs; Northern NGOs have identified the 'real lack of capacity' in Southern NGOs and Southern NGOs complain about the lack of motivation and capacity of the community groups with whom they work.

Capacity-building needs are across this chain. Rather than wishing this chain away or looking for ways to break it, it may be more effective to accept its existence and work within it to see how the capacity can be built at different levels.

Building your own Capacity

Experience reveals that the level of the chain at which one can have most impact on capacity-building is actually at one's own level and more specifically in one's organisation (just as in a personal relationship the only person one can change is oneself). We are much better able to build our own capacity than we are trying to build someone else's for them.

To some degree the funding system militates against Northern NGOs being too concerned with their own capacity-building. Northern NGOs are funded for their expertise and solutions; they are not funded for their own learning and capacity-building. As a result Northern NGOs need to be seen to be building others capacity, not their own.

This difficult funding system masks more deep-rooted issues in the Northern mind set. Despite the increasing distance from colonial days a pervasive paternalism still predominates. Examples of real mutual capacity-building and learning by the North are still the exception. To a degree it comes back to the underlying values and understanding of development. For the North a welfare approach to development is still much easier. There is more money for this and it does not fundamentally challenge the North's role.

The Challenge to Northern NGOs

The challenge to this comfortable Northern NGO existence is coming not only from the South with voices such as IFCB, but also from the corporate sector. Businesses tend to be more open about their interests then international NGOs, which is making for more open and transparent partnerships between businesses, such as Allied Dunbar/ZFS, and local NGOs.

It is increasingly clear though that for Northern NGOs to have effective impact through Southern NGOs there must be productive and trusting relationships in this aid chain. In the IFCB survey the top priority issues for North-South co-operation were relationship problems rather than programme matters. Where huge disparities in wealth, power and resources are perceived, 'as in the case of many African NGOs, problems of trust, respect and dependence may dominate the relationship even when the parties have good intentions, and for NGOs with more diversified access to resources, such as many Asian NGOs, the relationship difficulties may focus on negotiating shared values, goals and diagnoses of development problems'.

Productive relationships can only be developed when the North recognises the primary contributions made by their partners in the South. The lip-service which is paid to such notions is often belied by the underlying attitudes of paternalism – that we know best - which is perpetuated on a daily basis by the aid system in which we work. For real development to occur, such deep-rooted attitudes must be challenged and changed on an organisational and individual level, including in me.

Chapter 9

Implications for International NGOs in Developing Capacity-Building Strategies

Many Northern NGOs have prioritised capacity-building as one of their key strategies for the future, but have no coherent capacity-building approach. Their capacity-building interventions are still ad hoc and unco-ordinated with limited learning from experience in other countries[31]. Many are now feeling the need to take a more coherent and strategic approach to capacity-building. This final section is focused on helping these organisations get to grips with the process and issues involved in developing a coherent direction in capacity-building.

This publication has highlighted a number of lessons which such NGOs should incorporate into any capacity-building strategy.

Some of the lessons include the following:

EXPLORE AND ARTICULATE YOUR OWN AGENDA IN CAPACITY-BUILDING

Why are you really wanting to be involved in capacity-building? As with anything there will be a mixture of motives. As well as the more obvious altruistic motives, what unconscious interests are you serving? A desire to prove value added to donors? A justification for spending money on field offices? A desire to be directly involved in facilitating grass-roots development rather than just being an office-bound banker writing cheques and then policing? Unless you are honest with yourself about your motives and open with others, you will run the risk of seeing the impact of your well-meaning capacity-building programme undermined. Your own hidden agendas may well surface during the process, removing client ownership.

---

[31] There are notable exceptions to this picture and some NGOs are consciously addressing such issues, employing staff especially to bring coherence and direction to their capacity-building.

ANALYSE THE GLOBAL AND LOCAL CONTEXT THOROUGHLY

We have also seen how pervasive the impact of the context is on any capacity-building programme. **Contextual factors should be examined, both at a global level and at a local level.** The analysis of the global context of NGO capacity-building should help you understand how major global trends are influencing and directing your programme and thereby assist you in answering the question, 'capacity-building for what?'.

A good capacity-building strategy should also include provision for a detailed analysis of the local context (in developing specific programmes). The cases showed that the local context determined the nature of the internal capacity-building needs; the appropriateness of different capacity-building interventions; and the impact of the capacity-building programme. Understanding the local context means understanding how the past and current political, cultural, social and technological environments affect NGOs and capacity-building. It means exploring the local responses of government, NGOs and other actors to the global changes. It involves doing an assessment of the nature of demand from clients for capacity-building. It also involves investigating the supply profile of capacity-building providers in that area in terms of types, variety of services, perceptions of quality and relations between suppliers.

KEEP THE CARDINAL RULE OF CLIENT OWNERSHIP

Ensure that your **strategy does not break the cardinal rule of client ownership**. The most important factor in determining the success or otherwise of a capacity-building programme is the extent to which it is owned by the client. The whole approach of the programme from needs identification, intervention design, choice of provider, reporting procedures ... should be designed with this rule firmly in mind.

EXPLORE OPTIONS FOR STIMULAITNG DEMAND

At first glance, it might appear that this prevents a Northern NGO from any role in suggesting the need for capacity-building. This is not the case. There are a number of options which Northern NGOs have at their disposal for stimulating demand for capacity-building without removing ownership. You can **stimulate the demand of their partners for capacity-building** through:

1. **Bringing awareness of what capacity-building is**. This might be done through general trainings, introductory workshops or written information.

2. **Making partners aware of potential capacity-building providers** in their area. Some Southern NGOs do not have access to such information and merely the awareness that there is a capacity-building product on the market can stimulate demand.

3. **Funding budget lines for capacity-building** or even specific interventions can stimulate demand as a lack of resources often inhibits partners from identifying the need for and sourcing such services.

4. **Discussing, dialoguing and even negotiating** with partners about the need for capacity-building. This is a bit more directive and runs more risk of not being owned by the partner, but in healthy relationships this can be an effective tool. It tends to be better received when the Northern NGO is prepared to admit its own weaknesses and make itself part of the capacity-building process.

5. Another way of stimulating demand is to **trigger a crisis** in the NGO by withholding or removing funding. Financial crisis is sometimes the only thing that will force an NGO to change and improve (or die!). Triggering crisis is a very high risk strategy which can be abused to be very manipulative. It has to be used with thorough understanding of the organisation and great care, but it is a potentially 'developmental' intervention for a donor.

6. All these interventions are aided by ensuring that there is **co-operation** and consistent messages being sent by **other donors**. If donors send mixed messages the demand for capacity-building can be confused or dissipated.

DEVELOPING THE SUPPLY OF CAPACITY-BUILDING SERVICES

There are also a number of options **for Northern NGO strategies to work on the supply side of capacity-building**. For effective NGO capacity-building there need to be effective local providers of such services. Northern NGOs can work with these local providers in a number of ways:

1. You can **subsidise local capacity-building providers**. Charging full-cost

recovery fees for capacity-building services may not be feasible in all NGO sectors, especially in emerging sectors where NGOs are small and budgets are extremely limited. Furthermore, for capacity-building providers to really offer quality services requires investment in systematic organisational learning, the costs of which may not be possible to pass on to clients.

2. Another way in which Northern NGOs can stimulate the supply of local capacity-building services is to **contract local providers**. This offers the benefit of making the providers more market driven, but the question arises as to which market is driving – the Northern donor market or the Southern clients.

3. A less dangerous option is to **build the capacity of local providers**. This is aimed at individual local consultants or capacity-building institutions. For example, the donors agenda in the CDS/CRDT case was to build the capacity of CDS.

4. Another option taken by a number of Northern NGOs is to **create local providers**. Northern NGOs have recognised the problems of ownership inherent in providing capacity-building services themselves and so create local, entirely independent organisations to supply the sector with the required services.

5. A final option in increasing the supply of capacity-building services is for **Northern NGOs to provide these services directly themselves**. This is still the option favoured by many Northern NGOs as it gives them a hands-on role, but the funding link is likely to undermine authentic ownership and gives an incentive to cosmetic change. Where you have no funding links with the partners then this is much less of an issue. Where the capacity-building interventions are at fairly non-sensitive levels such as technical training in programme areas or financial management for example, then the mixed roles are also less of a problem. However, where the capacity-building needs are in sensitive areas, such as identity, leadership and strategy, then the presence of the controller of resources will undoubtedly distort and manipulate the process.

EMPOWER THE PARTNERS TO CHOOSE

If both demand for capacity-building and the supply of such services are there, it is still important that a Northern NGO's capacity-building strategy ensures that the Southern NGO client is given the **power to choose** which provider. If the Northern NGO selects the appropriate provider then the intervention will still be likely to be seen as a donor imposition, even if it were requested by the Southern NGO in the first place.

COMPROMISE ACCOUNTABILITY BEFORE OWNERSHIP

A Northern NGO strategy on capacity-building must also address the very real tension between the **need for confidentiality** in the primary relationship between provider and client and the **need to measure the impact** of the capacity-building programme. To ensure trust is maintained there should be no direct contact between the provider of the capacity-building and the ultimate payer. Any reports of capacity-building must be confidential to the client. If the NGO wishes to share such information with the donor that is a bonus, not a requirement, otherwise there would be incentives for the client to hide real problems which need confronting. Donors have to be prepared to fund and let go of the process. If you try and maintain a measure of control, there will be a direct trade-off in terms of less local ownership and more superficial change.

DEVELOP CREATIVE MONITORING AND EVALUATION MECHANISMS

As was shown in the previous chapter, however, there is a pressing need for Northern NGOs to develop creative ways of gauging whether their capacity-building investments have had any impact, without relying on confidential reports. While some work has gone on in this field, the conclusion from research into NGOs and capacity-building over five years ago stated that '**evaluation of capacity-building programmes** by NGOs is extremely limited and there is little evidence from NGOs regarding the effectiveness of their programmes'[32] still unfortunately largely holds true today.

---

[32] R. James, 1994, 'Strengthening the Capacity of Southern NGOs'.

MAKE STRATEGIC CHOICES OVER INTERVENTION POINTS

Other issues which Northern NGOs should consider in developing a capacity-building strategy is **at what level they are choosing to intervene** – the level of individuals; organisations; between organisations; and societal. Do you want to focus exclusively on one level? Do you want to use the first intervention as an entry point to gradually intervene at other levels? Do you wish to intervene at all levels simultaneously? Similarly with the **area of intervention**. Are you starting with a programme focus, an organisational focus or external relations focus? Do you wish to shift the capacity-building into other areas too, or concentrate on that one area? Where is the entry point and where is the ending point of your interventions? Each of these questions needs answering in developing capacity-building programmes based on a thorough analysis of the situation and the choices should be highlighted in the capacity-building strategy.

IMPLEMENT GOOD PRACTIVE LEARNINGS FROM OTHERS

Northern NGO capacity-building strategies should also seek to ensure that **good practice learnings** from capacity-building are fed into the design of specific programmes. A few of the good practice learnings which emerged from these cases include:

- the importance of leadership development in capacity-building and 'personalising' the capacity-building intervention;
- ensuring that the preconditions for ownership are there;
- the need to understand the power dynamics within organisations;
- clear, but different stakeholder roles;
- generous and arms-length donors; and
- interventions which are flexible, include follow-through, are participatory and provide incentives to change.

As well as integrating these learnings, it is of benefit to have an 'experiential learning' approach to capacity-building, taking innovative directions and consciously learning, documenting and disseminating experience.

MAKE YOUR SELF PART OF THE CAPACITY-BUILDING PROCESS

The case studies have also revealed the importance **of Northern NGOs being part of the capacity-building** programme themselves. Such an approach needs integrating into a capacity-building strategy in which it is understood that development impact is a function of the performance of different actors throughout the aid chain and not just the SNGO on its own. Northern NGOs must be prepared to admit their own capacity-building needs and change themselves, letting go of the profound, but often subconscious paternalism which says 'we are fine, you have the problem.'

Part of this capacity-building need involves Northern NGOs building their own capacity to implement their capacity-building strategy. To make such strategies achieve the results intended, Northern NGOs may need to address deficiencies of skills, systems and structures which would otherwise undermine their programme.

MAKE POWER SHIFTS YOUR GOAL

Be prepared to analyse and even to shift power relations. Stakeholders involved in capacity-building must become aware of their own power in the programme and how it influences the process. The power of control over resources must be recognised and accepted and yet, both in the North and the South, other sources of power such as being a locally accepted actor in civil society must also be recognised. Northern NGOs in supporting capacity-building of Southern partners must be prepared to accept and even welcome power shifts in the relationship. In fact a change in the power dynamics between Northern NGO and the Southern NGO may be one of the most potent and useful indicators of capacity being built. Northern NGO capacity-building strategies should not see power shifts as a threat, but as the very goal they are aiming for.

Bibliography

Allied Dunbar, 1997, 'The India Programme Social Accounting Report (1994–1996)'.

AIAMED / OI-India, 1998, 'A Will Needing a Way: Legal and Procedural Constraints in Micro-Finance'.

Andersson, G., 1998, 'Unbounded Organisations' unpublished.

Bebbington, A., and Mitlin, D., 1996, 'NGO Capacity-Building and Effectiveness: A Review of NGO-Related Research Projects Recently Funded by ESCOR', IIED.

Blunt, P., and Jones, M., 1992, *Managing Organisations in Africa*. Berlin: de Gruyter Studies in Organisation.

Blunt, P., 1995, The Cultural Limits of Process Consulting in Development Assistance', in R. Reineke and R. Sulzer (eds.) *Management Consultancy in Developing Countries. Berlin: Gabler.*

British Council, 1992, CRDT/CDS Higher Education Link memorandum.

British Council, 1996, CRDT/CDS Higher Education Link memorandum.

Burke, W., 1987, *Organization Development*. Reading, Mass: Addison-Wesley OD Series.

Campbell, P., 1994, 'What on Earth is OD Anyway'. WUS Directory Training, London.

Castillo, G. T. , 1997, 'Research Partnerships: Issues, Lessons, Results and Dreams for Sustainable Development'. AgREN, Network Paper No. 71: London, Overseas Development Institute.

CDRA Annual Report, 1996/7, 'Paradoxes of Power'.

CDS, 1997, 'Organisational Effectiveness from a Gender Perspective: Training Materials and Workshop Documentation' (unpublished).

CDS and CRDT, 1998, 'Organisational Effectiveness from a Gender Perspective'. Report of a workshop in Sayeda Zeinab, Cairo (unpublished).

Chambers, R., 1994, 'Participatory Rural Appraisal (PRA): Challenges, Potential and Paradigm'. World Development, 22/10: 1437–54.

CRDT and CDS, 1998, 'End of Link Evaluation Report'. British Council (unpublished).

Clayton, A., 1996, NGOs, *Civil Society and the State*. INTRAC.

Croal, P., 2000, 'Traditional Ecological Knowledge (TEK) and its Integration into CIDA Programming'. Policy Branch, CIDA.

Crockett, P., 1996, 'OD Useful in Changing Times: Interview with Allan Kaplan', Mott Exchange 10/3 (Dec.). Flint: Charles Stewart Mott Foundation.

149

Drucker, P. F., 1990, *Managing the Non-Profit Organisation – Principles and Practices*: New York: HarperCollins.

D'Souza, A., 'Being a Leader', Africa Christian Press.

Fowler, A., Jan. 2000, presentation at INGO Training programme, Arusha, Tanzania.

Fowler, A., Campbell, P., and Pratt, B., 1992, *Institutional Development and NGOs in Africa: Policy Perspectives for European Development Agencies*. Oxford: INTRAC.

Fowler, A., 1997, *Striking the Balance*. London: Earthscan.

Garbutt, A., 1997/8, INTRAC internal reports.

Garbutt, A., and Sinclair, M., 1998, 'NGOs in Uzbekistan', INTRAC.

Goold, E., Ogara, W., and James, R., 1998, 'Churches and Organisation Development in Africa: Directions and Dilemmas for NNGOs', INTRAC and CORAT Africa.

Handy, C., 1992, 'Balancing Corporate Power: A New Federalist Paper'. *Harvard Business Review*, (Nov/Dec).

Hatch, M. J., 1997, *Organization Theory: Modern Symbolic and Post-modern Perspectives*. Oxford.

Hesselbein, F., Beckard, R., eds., *Leader of the Future*. Drucker Foundation, Marshall Goldsmith.

Huse, E., and Cummings, T., 1985, *Organization Development and Change*. New York: West.

Info-Line, 1988, 'Organisational Development: What Trainers Need to Know', *American Society for Training and Development*, Issue 812 (Dec.).

INTRAC, 1998, 'Direct Funding from a Southern Perspective: Strengthening Civil Society?'. NGO Management and Policy Series No. 8, INTRAC.

James, R., 1994, 'Strengthening the Capacity of Southern NGOs', INTRAC.

James, R., 1998, *'Demystifying Organisation Development: Practical Capacity-Building Experiences of African NGOs'*, INTRAC

James, R., Ryder, P., and Elliott, S., 1998, 'Survey of Northern NGO Approaches to Capacity-Building'. IWGCB.

James, R., 1999, 'Up Close and Personal'. OD Debate, Olive, Durban.

Jamieson, N., 1987, The Paradigmatic Significance of Rapid Rural Appraisal. KKU Proceedings of the 1985 International Conference on Rapid Rural Appraisal, Thailand. 89–102.

Jorgensen, L., 1996, 'What are NGOs doing in Civil Society?', in A. Clayton (ed.), *NGOs, Civil Society and the State: Building Democracy in Transitional Societies*. INTRAC.

Kaplan, A, 1995, 'Closing Report of TTO Organisational Intervention'. August, CDRA.

Kisare, M., 1996, 'Fear and Abuse of OD'. Unpublished essay, EASUN.

Kotter, J., 1995, 'Leading Change: Why Transformation Efforts Fail', *HBR*, March–April, 59–67.

Mellon, T., 1997/8, INTRAC internal reports.

Mellon T., 1998, *NGOs in Kyrgyzstan*. INTRAC.

Morgan, P., and Qualman, A., 1996, 'Institutional and Capacity Development: Results-Based Management and Organisation Performance':CIDA, Feb.

Moser, C., 1993, *Gender Planning and Development: Theory, Practice and Training*. London: Routledge.

Muchunguzi, D., and Milne, S., 1995, 'Perspectives from the South: A Study on Partnership'. AFREDA.

Mugambi, J.N.K., (ed.), *The Church and Reconstruction of Africa: Theological Considerations*, All Africa Conference of Churches.

Pierce, D., 1994, 'End of Link Evaluation Report': CRDT, University of Wolverhampton (unpublished).

Pratt, B., and Goodhand J., 1996, 'Institutional Development of NGOs in Central Asia'. (DSA conference).

PRIA, 1998, 'Politics of Capacity Building' International Forum on Capacity Building, South and East Asia Consultation, Society for Participatory Research in Asia and International Institute of Rural Reconstruction.

Ramsden, P., 1994, *Learning to Teach in Higher Education*. London: Routledge.

Rao, A., and Kelleher, D., 1995, 'Engendering Open Change: The BRAC Case'. Eurostep Conference, Jan.

Reed, L., 1999, 'Breaking the Glass Wall', Opportunity International Network.

Riddell, R., and Bebbington, A., 1995, 'Developing Country NGOs And Donor Governments: Report to the ODA'. ODI.

Robinson, S., and Biersteker, L., (eds.) 1997, 'First Call: The South African Children's Budget'. IDASA Publications.

Schein, E., 1988, *Process Consultation: (Vol I) Its Role in Organisational Development*. Reading, Mass.: Addison Wesley OD Series.

Sweetman, C., (ed.)., 1997, Gender in Development Organisations. Gender and Development. 5/1 (Feb.) Oxford: Oxfam.

Transform, 1998, 'The Harare Declaration. Challenging Relationships: Redressing the Power Imbalances between Northern and Southern NGOs'.

Walters, P., 1990, 'Characteristics of Successful Organisational Development: A review of the literature', in *1990 Annual: Developing Human Resources*, Pfeiffer, University Associates.

Zurich Financial Services Community Trust Ltd., 2000, 'The India Programme Social Accounting Report (1997–1999)'.

151

Related INTRAC Titles

Autonomy or Dependence?
Case Studies of North-South NGO Partnerships
Vicky Mancuso Brehm with Emma Harris-Curtis, Luciano Padrão and Martin Tanner
£15.95 ISBN 1-897748-74-4 207pp 2004

This book explores the concept and practice of 'partnership' between non-government organisations (NGOs) in the North and South. Based on a rigourous four-year study, the book draws together the perspectives of a group of European NGOs and compares these with the experiences of their partners in Brazil, Cambodia and Tanzania. The authors look ahead to how partnerships are changing as networks and alliances of Northern and Southern civil society organisations join together to work on common issues.

Capacity Building from a French Perspective
Mia Sorgenfrei
Praxis Papers 1 £5.95 ISBN 1-897748-85-X 40pp July 2004 French version ISBN 1-897748-87-6 44pp 2004

This paper depicts how French NGOs perceive the notion of capacity building, and how they apply the concept in practice. It provides a synthesis of current capacity building needs, trends and challenges in France and in the South. Capacity building is perceived by French NGOs as an Anglophone concept. However, NGOs have had little exposure to Anglophone approaches to capacity building, and there is scope for more exchange in the future.

People and Change
Exploring Capacity Building in NGOs
Rick James
NGOMPS 15 £15.95 ISBN 1-897748-68-X 161pp 2002

Based on many years of practical experiences with NGOs, largely in Africa, this book argues that for capacity building programmes to be more effective we must: better appreciate the complex and highly personal dimensions to organisational change; understand the culture and context within which the capacity building takes place and adjust the programmes accordingly; consciously learn from our capacity building work by taking the monitoring and evaluation of our work much more seriously. Using a mixture of case studies, illustrations from experiences and articles based on reflective practice, People and Change provides practitioners with ideas, suggestions and challenges to improve the effectiveness of the capacity building interventions.

Partnerships: Negotiating Relationships
A Resource for Non-Governmental Development Organisations
Alan Fowler
Occasional Papers Series 32 £8.95 ISBN 1-897748-57-4 25pp 2000

To order please contact INTRAC Publications, PO Box 563, Oxford, OX2 6RZ, UK.
Tel: +44 (0) 1865 201851 Fax: +44 (0) 1865 201852 E-mail: publications@intrac.org